"These short discourses by a~ ~ ~ ~ns
possible imminent death are re ~ ~endly in tone.
They speak directly to the heart of human suffering, the
confusion that comes from not understanding what is
clearly available for us to feel directly and be liberated. It
is a book I keep on my bedside table, at close hand when
I need a dose of encouragement." —**Sylvia Boorstein,
cofounding teacher of Spirit Rock Meditation Center
and author of** *Happiness Is an Inside Job*

"Life is amazing when we step out of our thoughts, our
selves, and become the mystery alive to itself. With kindness and Zen directness, Yoshin David Radin opens the
gate of simplicity and invites us to live here, awake, free."
—**Jack Kornfield, author of** *No Time Like the Present*

"'You should find your salvation by becoming bored
with your suffering...if you can be alone with yourself,
you can be comfortable anywhere.' With such unexpected and unpretentious teachings, Yoshin David Radin
makes Zen completely available. *A Temporary Affair* is
a treasure house of comforting wisdom, a book you'll
go back to again and again to undo the tangles in your
mind."—**Norman Fischer, poet, Zen priest, and author
of** *The World Could Be Otherwise: Imagination and the
Bodhisattva Path*

"This is a wonderful book. It is simple. It is clear. There are poetic moments. But, bottom line, Yoshin David Radin speaks to us from the heart of the matter. Here is a Zen life as an authentic life. I highly recommend it." —**James Ishmael Ford, author of** *Introduction to Zen Koans: Learning the Language of Dragons*

"With warmth, humor, and gentle authority, Zen teacher Yoshin David Radin shares the fruits of decades of intimacy with the mind to invite us home to the heart. His very real proximity to his own death charges these dharma talks with a kind of tender beauty that touched me to my core." —**Mirabai Starr, author of** *Wild Mercy: Living the Fierce and Tender Wisdom of the Women Mystics* **and** *God of Love: A Guide to the Heart of Judaism, Christianity and Islam*

"Do we really need another book on Buddhism? YES! But only if that book and collection of talks is Yoshin David Radin's *A Temporary Affair*. Sitting with this book is like sitting with a roshi and having the wisdom within you mirrored back to you in a way that shatters everything that keeps you from knowing who you are and aren't. Read this book slowly. The talks may be casual, but the truth is anything but." —**Rabbi Rami Shapiro, author of** *The Tao of Solomon: Unlocking the Perennial Wisdom of Ecclesiastes* **and** *Judaism Without Tribalism: A Guide to Being a Blessing to All the Peoples of the Earth*

"This is a collection of genuine teachings from the heart that resonate with an authenticity that comes from Yoshin

David Radin's many years of practice. It is both profound and practical, a fine line that few Zen teachers are able to walk." —**Hal Roth, professor of religious studies and director of the Contemplative Studies Initiative at Brown University**

"Reading these talks by Yoshin David Radin is sharing one's life with a wise and kind old friend. With his gentle words he dissolves the ridges of the boundaries we presume in our life. With simple words and common images Yoshin shares his experience of dissolving distracted mind, and thereby reveals the boundless heart that is our common unity." —**Seiju Bob Mammoser, senior teacher at the Albuquerque Zen Center**

"Yoshin David Radin shares with all of us his deep insight. He knows what it means to take up the study and practice of Zen. He offers a way to live life through the clear lens of reality, and his words reflect those of Huang Po: 'the ignorant reject what they see, not what they think; the wise reject what they think, not what they see.' Yoshin has a poignant insider's view. It should open many a wayfarer's eyes." —**Hwalson Sunim, abbot of the Detroit Zen Center**

"Reading this book of Yoshin's simple, elegant Zen teachings, tears come—tears of gratitude for his generous encouragement, tears that recognize what is deeply true. He teaches us to sit and walk in courage, humility, and grace, as long as we live." —**Trudy Goodman, founding teacher at InsightLA**

"In this very clear, straightforward and helpful guide to Zen meditation, Yoshin David Radin is generous and welcoming in his approach to the dharma. He is also strong in insisting on the temporary nature of this reality and nonpermanent self. Dharma practice is seen by Yoshin as a spiritual path to uncover our own true nature, which is profoundly good and unified with all that exists.

"While not religious, this view echoes mystical teachings in many traditions. I was especially moved by the healing of Yoshin's relationship with his orthodox Jewish mother on her deathbed when she says to him, 'You've been living in heaven these past few years, haven't you?' This is a poignant moment and testimony to the dharma practice." —**Rabbi Sheila Peltz Weinberg, author of** *God Loves the Stranger*

"In this book, those who are investigating the human condition will find a cornucopia of food for thought and heartwarming expression shared by a fellow human, well versed in living and equally adept in dying. Yoshin's students collected these talks and made them available to us with his help. Great hearts sharing: Wonderful!" —**Dokurō R. Jaeckel, abbot of Charles River Zen Center**

"If you're reading this, you've found something very special. There are many individuals who, from the generosity and wisdom of their insights, attempt to share their hard-won understanding with others. The challenge is that Zen insights don't pack easily into language and the results often read like cliché. I recommend that you keep this book by your bedside and savor a few pages each night. You will experience the delight of finding something very subtle captured in words. The articulation found in this collection is a humble gift." —**Jerry Mirskin, poet, professor at Ithaca College, and author of** *Crepuscular Non Driveway*

"Yoshin was experiencing life-threatening health issues while giving talks in *A Temporary Affair*, which adds great poignancy to his words, as if to say: 'This is real; I'm not kidding around.' Yet despite his stark confrontation with mortality, he conveys dharma wisdom with a lightness of heart and gentle humor that is astounding and extremely useful for any of us who plan to die at some point.

"As someone who thought he was possibly approaching the end of life, this is not merely a nice, spiritual idea; it was Yoshin's potentially final offering of love and compassion, a much-needed reminder that there is a way out for all of us." —**Eliezer Sobel, author of** *Minyan: Ten Jewish Men in a World That Is Heartbroken*, **and** *The 99th Monkey: A Spiritual Journalist's Misadventures*

ALSO BY

Yoshin David Radin

Love Songs of a Zen Monk
May It Be So
Deathbed Lullaby
Ever Since I Met You
I Am With You

A
Temporary
Affair

TALKS ON AWAKENING AND ZEN

David Radin

Monkfish Book Publishing
Rhinebeck, New York

A Temporary Affair: Talks on Awakening and Zen © 2022 by David Radin

Paperback ISBN 978-1-948626-67-5
eBook ISBN 978-1-948626-68-2

Library of Congress Cataloging-in-Publication Data

Names: Radin, David, 1946- author.
Title: A temporary affair : talks on awakening and Zen / David Radin.
Description: Rhinebeck : Monkfish Book Publishing Company, 2022.
Identifiers: LCCN 2021060917 (print) | LCCN 2021060918 (ebook) | ISBN
    9781948626675 (paperback) | ISBN 9781948626682 (ebook)
Subjects: LCSH: Spiritual life--Buddhism. | Dharma (Buddhism) | Zen
    Meditations. | Zen Buddhism.
Classification: LCC BQ9289.5 .R335 2022 (print) | LCC BQ9289.5 (ebook) |
    DDC 294.3/444--dc23/eng/20211228
LC record available at https://lccn.loc.gov/2021060917
LC ebook record available at https://lccn.loc.gov/2021060918

Book design by Colin Rolfe
Front cover photo by Kurt Brand
Author photo by Kathy Morris

Monkfish Book Publishing Company
22 East Market Street, Suite 304
Rhinebeck, NY 12572
(845) 876-4861
monkfishpublishing.com

There is no insight that compares
to seeing the emptiness of names and forms

There is no happiness that compares
to seeing the mind awaken from its fall into thinking

There is no sadness that compares
to seeing the suffering of mind lost in individuality

There is no compassion that compares
to seeing the true self in all

There is no love that compares
to seeing the oneness of all existence

— Yoshin David Radin

Contents

Dedication and Introduction

This book is a collection of talks I gave during Sunday morning sittings at the Ithaca Zen Center. The talks were given between 2017 and 2019, at a time when my health was severely compromised by end-stage renal failure. Serious heart and blood pressure complications led to several late-night dashes to the emergency room.

In February 2019 I received a kidney transplant from a member of the Ithaca Zen Center, Sue Smith, to whom this publication is dedicated. The incredible generosity of body and spirit that she manifested created a remarkable atmosphere of lovingkindness that permeates the Ithaca Zen Center to this day.

Deep thanks to Richard Faria, who transcribed the talks and whose energy was responsible for producing the book.

And to my wife and teachers, who obviously are responsible for the content herein.

May these pages help provide some insight into the deeper spiritual view.

Preface

In this collection of talks, Yoshin David Radin points us toward a more direct experience of our deeper nature and does so with humor, a warm heart, and penetrating insight. The teachings range from taking care of the mind in everyday life by realizing that no external or psychological object or experience can bring lasting satisfaction, to seeing into the wonder of the Great Truth. And because these insights lie within all of us, because they are fundamentally simple, they are accessible to all. They need only to be pointed out.

I first met Yoshin while finishing my undergraduate degree. He had been invited by the Jewish Chaplain of the college to lead a series of "Introduction to Meditation" classes. I had a classmate who was interested, so I tagged along. A handful of students assembled in the college chapel and the abbot and founder of the Ithaca Zen Center (a rural Zen practice community about eight miles south of Ithaca, New York) Yoshin showed us some basics of how to find a comfortable seat, and where to rest our hands. He gave us a simple breath counting practice and then began a period of meditation. After twenty-five minutes or so, he rang a bell and said, with a conspiratorial grin, "Any questions?"

I had so many questions! Chief among them was how I had gotten this far in my life and never looked at the content of my own mind. I sat quietly with nothing but my own thoughts, something I had never been asked to do before, and was horrified by the chaos I discovered.

I attended the remaining classes in the series, but graduated soon after, and with the business of final exams and my preparing to relocate to continue my education, I never got a chance to thank Yoshin for showing me what was right under my own nose. I continued a meditation practice as I traveled around, but always fondly remembered Yoshin's ability to convey subtle and esoteric aspects of the Dharma as simple common sense, and with a gentle good humor.

I returned to my undergraduate college some ten years later to take a faculty position, and one of my first orders of business was to look up Yoshin and pick up my meditation practice where I had left off with him. In the intervening time I attended the weekly sittings and sesshins (weeklong retreats) that he has led at the Ithaca Zen Center, and always found his teachings inspiring and moving. His talks were tailored in the moment to the people in attendance and the occasion or time of year, and had a perfection of form, depth of insight, and an artless poetry that merited repeated listening. Over time it became apparent that these talks were not prewritten or planned out, but rather channeled from some deeper wisdom. I thought it would be wonderful to have these talks in written form so that the more subtle passages that might evade a first hearing could be reread for deeper understanding, but I lacked the courage to ask for permission to record them. I also knew how putting a microphone in front of a speaker can make them self-censor.

I eventually got up the courage to ask him if I might record some of his talks, and while he didn't understand why anyone would care to listen to him sell water by the river, he consented. My thinking was that I would some-day transcribe the recordings for him to edit as a collection, though he knew nothing of this plan. It was shortly after I began recording that he announced to the sangha that he was in the later stages of kidney failure and was not sure how much longer he would be able to continue leading retreats and giving talks. In the moment, I didn't know what to think, so I just carried on recording. As his health began to fail, the talks became more transcendent, and I recorded right up until the days before he was admitted to the hospital for a transplant. That order of talks is mostly preserved in this collection.

To avoid bogging down this book with footnotes, it might be helpful to define a few terms and concepts as Yoshin uses them in his talks.

Five Skandhas: The five components of ego structure.
Grace: Ultimately, the release from suffering.
Jiki: Short for Jikijitsu, the person who leads the meditation hall and monitors the sitting times.
Mind Training: Guiding the mind to function without causing suffering to itself or others.
Practice: Specific activities to train the mind and cultivate lovingkindness.
Sangha: The Buddhist community of monks, nuns, novices, and laity.
Sesshin: A five-to-seven-day period of intensive meditation.
Shoji: The person who supports the wellbeing of the practitioners in the zendo.

Wisdom Lineage/Wisdom Teachings/Prajna Teachings:
The lineage that transmits the teachings about the true nature of the mind or being.

Zazen: Seated meditation.

Zen Practice: The practice of dissolving the self and bringing the mind to stillness and insight.

Zendo: A Zen meditation hall.

It has been an honor to be part of bringing these teachings of love and wisdom to a wider audience. May they ring the bell of the Dharma.

— Richard Faria

A Temporary Affair

*E*ACH ONE OF US WILL ONE DAY experience a day that has no tomorrow. Each one of us will experience an out-breath that is not followed by an in-breath. Each one of us will experience going to sleep on a night that has no morning. Or we will experience, one day, a morning that has no evening. This is the human condition, referred to as *impermanence*. To live with a deep acceptance of impermanence is to be a follower of the noble truth. Given that this is the human condition, how do you greet your last morning? How do you greet your last meeting with a friend? How do you greet your last sunset?

The capacity to experience objects is what it means to exist as an individual. A human being is the mind identifying itself as a human body experiencing objects. That identification is a temporary affair, a very temporary affair. In fact, this morning it looked like an extremely temporary affair. That's how it is these days. It is often only when impermanence touches you that the preciousness of being alive touches you. And if you don't realize the preciousness of being alive, you have to suffer worrying about whether someone loves you or not. This is the curse that you have to live under. If you realize the preciousness of being alive, everything else becomes insignificant.

Next time you hug a friend, thinking you may never have this opportunity again, you will really know what a hug is—the opportunity to melt in the arms of a friend, and suddenly the inner sun shines upon you. I hope you can realize the old teaching that a true student of Zen experiences more joy in the raising and lowering of an arm than a person who does not know the truth experiences in an entire lifetime. One moment, thoroughly present, relaxed and awake to the truth of the deeper illumination, makes one richer than a king.

You Will Be a Beacon

IT IS HARD TO EXPLAIN what spiritual practice is, what true spiritual life is. It is hard to explain because people's minds have become so deluded. When we grew up, we were never taught to question the meaning of life. We were never taught that we should understand why we are alive before we draw up our plan for how we should live. From the beginning we are force-fed a formula that life is about continually proving our worth, our worthiness of love; and it starts early—that we should be potty-trained, we should be the best kindergarten student, we should get the most gold stars—at the youngest possible age. We go to school, a system that is constantly pushing us to achieve, and nobody tells us to examine whether that is for our ultimate benefit—we are just told to do it. We are not told about impermanence. We are not told that personal life may be unfixable, that it inevitably contains failure and loss, and that there are conditions for being alive that, if ignored, will create suffering. This system may create huge problems.

I would like to suggest a new operating system for life. It is not something I made up; it is the operating system of the wisdom lineage. We should examine it because, ultimately, it is the only path to happiness and meaningfulness. It is the only way to integrate impermanence. It is the truth. It will help us to understand the fundamental dilemma—why there is stress in life, why there is fear in life, why life sometimes seems shallow, and why happiness is unstable.

The "enemy" is the mind looking outside itself for a solution. That mind is not taught that it is causing its own suffering. Instead, it has been trained to compete and struggle to attain something that will give it a feeling of fulfillment; a feeling that we should spend a whole life accomplishing something that is going to provide fulfillment, instead of realizing that fulfillment is innate. We were born fulfilled; we are as we are, and nothing we do in life can alter that. Personal victories provide only temporary satisfaction. We spend our time pursuing these temporary goals that we set for ourselves, thinking that they are meaningful and significant. We get aggressive toward things that frustrate us. When we lose, we blame external causes, when we have a relationship that is going sour, we blame the other person, when we have a career that takes an unexpected turn, we get angry at the circumstances.

This is how our mind responds, and it will help us to recognize that this way of thinking is the very enemy of happiness. How sad it is to look around and see people frustrated in life for no reason other than their own mistaken thinking! People get caught desperately wanting—wanting to have a relationship, wanting to have a career, wanting to have a specific thing happen—and it is not happening. They do not realize that it is the line of thinking that is painful; the situation has no inherent pain. The pain is created by the mind.

People want to be selfish, but they don't know how to be selfish skillfully. If we really had our own self-interest at heart, would we ever create anger? Would we ever allow such a horrible experience to come into the mind? No! Would we ever dislike ourselves? No! It would be absurd. Why would we introduce painful experiences into our minds? It is the same as going to a frying pan left on the stove with the heat on: grabbing hold of it and burning one's hand, then saying, "Well, I should throw out that frying pan, it hurt me, it's terrible. Stupid frying pan!" Please understand that this is human thinking.

The reason I mention all these things is to encourage you to take a path in life that is more noble, a path that acknowledges that no external object can fulfill you. This may allow yourself a certain freedom—the freedom to just relax in the present moment, to breathe, smile, and come back to yourself. There is no need to get rid of your neuroses—that is inflicting more struggle, more enmity, more aggression upon yourself and others. If you come to the zendo and you don't like yourself or your practice, it means that you are still experiencing aggression. You are still having a tendency to judge the way you are, or to reject the experiences you have had in life. That needs to be relaxed. When you become at ease with the totality of your current state of being, the totality of your life, you will become a beacon in the world. And when you can love yourself and forgive yourself and have a sense of humor about how ridiculous you are, you will become a beacon.

All of us can be beacons when we change how we look at life. Instead of seeing a battleground where we must achieve something, just walk across the lawn knowing that you are completely fulfilled as you are walking. There is no higher state than the one you are in right now; you just haven't been with yourself in a while. So please, stay in touch with your own well-being, instead of thinking it is in the future. That is what you can uncover in your meditation practice.

All Peace Breaks Loose

WOULD LIKE TO TALK this morning about the basics of zazen practice—to clarify, if possible, the basics of the actual practice of zazen. So that when you sit down to practice, you don't have to deal with any doubt or question about what to do. Even though it is actually impossible to explain, I'd like to try anyway.

The difficulty people have in zazen practice is that they are coming into it with "I" residing in thinking. When that self tries to practice zazen, it thinks it has something to do with manipulating the thinking activity, assuming that peace comes through suppression of thought. But the practice of zazen is not performed by the thinking activity, so the self that you take yourself to be has nothing to do; there is nothing that needs to be done to, or with, the mind to practice zazen. The mind just is as it is. But we get caught in judging it, or using it, or daydreaming. We don't have any other tool besides the thinking activity if "I" is immersed in the thinking activity. This is the situation.

Please understand that if you are using the mind to practice zazen, you will never get far. Instead, what we are trying to do is to get out of the way to allow the awareness to penetrate the breathing activity; we are allowing the experience of our body breathing. We cannot produce that experience as a self in the thinking activity because thinking cannot be aware of breathing.

Thinking does not have to disturb if you just allow it to be and refrain from judging it or interacting with it. Another way of explaining allowing is *relaxing*. Instead of trying to work with the mind, bring your awareness to the body and make sure the shoulders are soft, the neck is upright but soft, the arms are soft, and the chest and belly are soft. In that softening of the body is the invitation to experience it; so that when your body is in harmony and the breathing is taking place as an activity, and you are relaxed, then the awareness of the breathing is more accessible. You are leaning into the physical feeling of the breathing activity. Thinking is going to disrupt that contact but reacting to such thinking is a mistake. Be prepared to allow the thinking to be as neurotic and distracting as it needs to be. There is no problem with the thinking activity except in wanting it to be other than the way it is. If you do not want thinking to be other than the way it is, then thinking will not bother you. Just be there, and after a short period of practice like that, you will be able to smile at the thinking activity.

The practice is to lean into the breathing activity. When Buddha described it, he said, *"Breathing in, there is the full penetrating awareness of breathing in, and when breathing out, there is the full penetrating awareness of breathing out."* Please understand that *you* cannot do that; *you* can only allow that by relaxing.

If you persevere in this way, the inner environment takes on a very different flavor from when you were struggling with the thinking activity. Suddenly, all peace breaks loose! You can start to see the path, and the path is that when you allow the awareness and the breathing to caress each other, to be intimate with each other, you will feel happy and clear and at ease. You will be engaging with the proper way to extract the self from the thinking activity: this is Zen practice. Will is not capable of suppressing thinking. So if your defense against negative thinking-states is to run from them or suppress them, you will never be safe because they will overpower you.

I was talking to a friend yesterday who is in a lot of physical pain. Not only was he in physical pain, but he also thought he could transcend it with his will. When he failed in that effort, he felt even worse.

Things are just as they are, and the only thing out of place is your will. The practice is to give up the fight with the thinking activity, to give up the fight with things as they are and come back home to your deeper state. It cannot be described, but you can hint at it by saying, "When breathing in, I am relaxed and aware of breathing in, when breathing out, I am relaxed and aware of breathing out." And when thinking disrupts, "I have nothing to say about that, that is your business. You are on your own."

Practice in this kind of way, and you will find sitting down to be a very welcoming state—there is no fight with the thinking activity. Your tendency toward aggression has been released. It is just, okay, you are free now to go roam. I am sitting at home, relaxed, and experiencing myself being relaxed.

Bearing the Pain and the Insult

WHAT ARE YOU LOOKING INTO when you take up the practice of Zen? Most religions are based on something supernatural, something extraordinary that took place outside of you. "Once upon a time there was a great prophet; once upon a time there was a great god." Or maybe if you are an atheist, "Once upon a time there was a big bang." I don't know if the big bang is God, but perhaps it works the same way: it is outside you. People approach religion, spirituality, the meaning of life by having a connection to something external that is glorious. In those traditions, if you want to have a connection to God, you have to go to a church, a priest or minister, or perhaps a physicist for that connection. Through that you plug into a channel that will allow what is called "religion" to come into your being.

Zen is based on an entirely different principle: that the meaning of your life has been inside you from the moment you were born. That which is going to make sense of your whole life is within you, it is not something that you can study outside. Almost no one has been informed of this. People have been informed that you will fulfill yourself through a successful career, through a successful family life, through wealth, through worship. All these things outside you are how your life is rated.

Why have we lost the connection to this fulfillment that is within us from the beginning? The reason is precisely because we have made outside circumstances more important than our inner content. We become dependent on how we look to others, we gain validation from others. When we gain validation from others, we disempower ourselves. We do not have any internal validation to draw on. Our inside has become polluted, our inside has become insulted by our way of life. We have not paid any attention to our state of mind because we are told to focus on external accomplishments. What that does to our emotions is tragic.

In order to cultivate inner spiritual strength, we need to recoup the power that we have granted to circumstances to determine our emotional state. Doesn't that make sense? Very simple, this Zen stuff: if you want to have a pleasant inner state, you should cultivate a pleasant inner state. But if you spend all your time cultivating external accomplishments, you ignore what is going on inside and what this external life is doing to you.

Meditation practice is not pleasant or easy at the beginning. People say you should meditate because you will find peace of mind. That is not what you find. The first thing you find when you take up meditation is that you are face to face with your own insanity. You will discover what has happened to your mind because you have not given it any attention: it is out of control. People leave meditation practice because they are unable to bear the pain and the insult. You have to learn what it is like to look at your mind and not judge it. That is the first stage of meditation practice—to be able to experience what is going on in there authentically. And this requires a significant amount of courage because it is easy to be discouraged by what is in there. But there is no other way.

If you want to find inner acceptance, inner kindness, inner softness, inner love, inner consciousness, the thinking mind will have to be experienced exactly how it is. That is why some people prefer a savior. A savior is designed to save you from the parts of your mind and the parts of your life that you cannot bear. So, if you are experiencing fear, you pray to be saved from fear; if you have depression, you pray to be saved from depression. But there is a path through these difficult states whereby one can save oneself. And that path is the radical, humble acceptance of the mind as it is. You may not have been told that before, and you may have squandered a lot of energy trying to prove yourself competent in the external environment. All that happens is that you grow old, and all of the things you have strived for disappear. Everything you have spent your energy on cannot survive the passage of time and the aging of the mind.

Whenever you realize, "I really need a deeper view of what's going on here, what I am committing myself to doesn't quite make sense," find a teacher who knows how to experience the mind unscathed. I encourage people to continue in meditation practice, but make sure that you have the proper attitude. Meditation is not like collecting wealth, collecting status, or having people say, "You're really good at this." No, meditation is based on deep humility; that is why there is a lot of bowing and gestures of respect in the practice. The mood that will protect you to go inside yourself and experience what is there without reacting to it has to be humble. Otherwise, you will bump into that which you reject or struggle with. The meditator has to go in and see what is there and not react. There is no other way. You are not judging yourself or getting down on yourself—you are being honest about yourself.

There will be a point when you will discover that there is an inner stability that has been with you all along, that there is something extraordinary that has been with you all along, and that is your own consciousness—the one who is inside and actually beholds the thinking activity. You don't yet know that part of yourself, but the one that goes in and sees the thinking activity and is not affected by it is that which will be with you all along and will never fail you.

Fellow Forms of the Most Miraculous Assembly

MOST PEOPLE DON'T KNOW that the *Jiki* (who sits at the head of the meditation hall) and I went to high school together. We even played on the same basketball team. Now we're just bench sitters! But we used to be players. You might wonder why I bring this up. Something significant happened in the world of basketball yesterday. A women's college team that had not lost for three years set the all-time record for consecutive wins—111 games in a row. And then they lost. That's the lesson.

One of the interesting things about sports is that when we win, we always thank God. When we lose, we don't thank God. "Thank God that other player made that shot and we lost!" No, mind doesn't work that way. Mind works this way: "God made the ball go in, and we won." Buddha realized something very fundamental to human life, which is that our last activity will be a loss. It will be a loss of the eyes, ears, nose, tongue, body, and mind. Every human being will experience that loss. And the question is, how do you live your life based on knowing that this is your final act? Shouldn't it be to practice how to lose?

One of the unfortunate things that can happen in life is to have a long winning streak. You start to think life is an endless conquest. We have been given the idea that life is a hill you are climbing, and on the top of the hill—I'm not sure what is there. Maybe it's a Rolls-Royce, maybe it's a house on the beach in Hawaii. We are on a path that consists of conquests and we do not accept loss—it is not integrated well. When people who are living a life like that grow old and start losing things, they lose their sense of humor because they have been taught that one is supposed to show up as a winner.

Sometimes people come into meditation thinking, "I've been doing this practice so that I can become an accomplished meditator." That is wrong, that is not what happens in meditation—you first realize how neurotic the mind is. You don't realize that you are a competent meditator, because as an individual, *you* are a mental activity, *you* are the very thing that makes meditation impossible, so how can *you* meditate?

When we come together as practitioners, we come together as brothers and sisters of impermanence. That is the bond that unites a sangha—that our stay here is impermanent, and we acknowledge that. When we are not self-absorbed, the beauty of a spring morning brings tears to the eyes. There is a sensitivity that existence is so transient, so miraculous, and so splendid.

I don't know if it is possible to appreciate quite how astonishing it is that the universe created out of itself the human body—out of water, earth, air, food, and a will-less chain of causation. These conditions have come together to evolve something that can see, hear, smell, taste, touch and think. It has evolved these incredible activities. To be able to see takes a complexity of structure that is unimaginable. To be able to smell—same. It is unimaginably complex how the brain and the nervous system evolved. The universe evolved this system so that it could experience what it was. The universe gave rise to something out of itself that could experience its own existence—that is what a human being is, that is why our existence is glorious.

But when we take this existence and turn it into self-importance, it is heartbreaking. If God could be offended, she would be. How could one take something so majestic and exquisite as this system, and become aggressive toward the very universe that gave rise to it out of itself? Please appreciate that the other people who are existing are all fellow forms of the most miraculous assembly of particles. And when we see each other with that feeling about life, we start to understand what "sacred" means. How sacred it is to *be*. You are a practitioner who understands that winning and losing are trivial; you have already won. You were born having won. Then, go forth into the universe to enjoy your victory, which is that the sun shines and that water quenches your thirst.

Saved from a Superficial Stay

PRACTICED WITH MY TEACHER for thirty-seven years until he passed away at one hundred and seven. He was old for a long time. When you live to be one hundred and seven, you are old for a long time. For many years, when I would go to see him, I would think, "I wonder if this is the last time I'm going to see him?" Sometimes I would cry. Later, I spent a few years going out to Los Angeles after he had passed away, and I would go to visit with my old friend Leonard Cohen. We'd look at each other and think, "Is this the last time we will see each other?" Of course, you don't know it is the last time until it is too late. But there was a sense of the last moment—that two old Zen brothers could look into each other's eyes and smile.

Nowadays, sometimes I wake up in the morning and look at myself and think, "How much longer will I be able to look in the mirror and see my old friend?" It's funny how life goes on. It was deeply precious to think that this was the last time I'd be seeing a teacher, or the last time seeing a brother, or the last time seeing this form that I live in. It is incredibly poignant. How many people take the time to experience their life in a deep, delicious way? How many times are we not too busy to experience a moment of profound gratitude for being here? When we are not being clever, and we are not looking for a job or looking for what is going to fulfill us, but just in the fullness of the moment—walking, talking, in the deep fullness of the moment.

This is, in a way, what mind training is designed to produce–the appreciation of our very existence, instead of mere use of existence to satisfy self-based desires–that we are appearing here with the precious body of a human being. And in this body, we all have the capability of realizing that there is a wisdom that transcends the ego and transcends the form of every creature that appears in this world.

This human body is, perhaps, the only form in which this insight is accessible—and it requires a very sophisticated system. A human being is more sophisticated than an amoeba, or a fish, or a dog. A human being is an astonishingly complex system. Not that there is a self in that system, it's not that the human being has a permanent self. A human being is a term given to the complex structure that has five skandhas. This thing that you are now existing as has eyes, ears, nose, tongue, body, and mind. And the mind is extremely sophisticated, more so than in any other creature. This mind, however, is used by most people in ways that are ridiculous, or in some cases even barbaric. It is being used to dominate others, to create destruction. No matter how angry a dog gets, it can only cause a limited amount of harm. But human beings, because of the sophistication of the mind, can hurt and destroy an entire ecosystem. If we are fortunate, we meet the Buddha dharma, which says, "Look closely into your own mind, and you will see that the bodymind does not contain a self." There is no other species that can contemplate its own existence in this way.

This is the invitation from the teachings—that we can be saved from a superficial stay here. We can be saved from the suffering produced by thinking that we are permanent individuals. If we introspect properly, we will see that everything inside this body is visible to penetrating awareness. When the awareness "penetrates" the mind and the body, the mind awakens from identifying its self incorrectly. "Penetrates" means experiences. We have the capacity to experience this bodymind. When we experience this bodymind, we can see that there is no unchanging element in it.

If we experience that there is no unchanging element within our personal existence—that we cannot hold anything forever, we cannot be anything forever—then stressing over circumstances becomes absurd. I'll say that again: Stressing over circumstances becomes absurd if you realize this insight, if you seriously look at your life. All you have to do is look back on your life, on all the things that mattered when you were a child, or as a teenager, or as an adult. You sweated over this and worried over that yet you can't even remember all those things that used to be so, so, significant. When you see yourself stressing over these things, say to yourself, "Don't worry, don't fret, don't worry at all. Don't torture yourself for no reason, it really is for no reason." And that is how it is for anything. People who are spiritually immature and inexperienced worry about all kinds of things. Whereas a spiritually mature mind knows that reacting to circumstances in a selfish way is pointless; that reactions to life can be born from a wisdom view. We have the capacity to respond to the circumstances of our life, knowing that the very response determines the quality of our life. The situation we respond to with selfishness creates emotional trouble.

The insights of the Zen way are very simple. If you respond selfishly, it is going to be painful. If you respond with a detached, clear mind, you will experience a detached, clear, grateful life. When you are sitting in zazen, you are cultivating the quality of not reacting to your mental content, so that when thinking arises, it is just thinking. It has no particular meaning or form; it is not something that you have to respond to. That is called cultivating tranquility, and it will be to your great benefit. You will see people getting upset about circumstances because they have no sense of cultivating tranquility. People react, "Oh, this is so hard, the political scene in America now is so hard." This is how the mind is reacting to the circumstances. There have been times in the history of humanity when monks were gathered out of temples and slaughtered. There were times when Jews were gathered out of their temples and slaughtered— and times when Kurdish people were slaughtered, times when Armenian people were slaughtered, times when Indigenous Americans were slaughtered, Chinese were slaughtered, Japanese were slaughtered, Russians were slaughtered. The human species can be horrible. For the quality of your life to be at the mercy of a political system means that you have not taken impermanence to heart.

That is tranquility practice. People new to practice will notice that the tranquility element is quite lacking. You can feel that. And the mind is unleashed in zazen practice. You don't have the normal stimuli; you are left alone with your mind. And most people are uneasy when left alone with their minds. They don't know how to be comfortable with the tantrums and insanities that go on in the mind. It is normal for the mind to be unbalanced when its props are pulled out from under it. So know that enduring the tantrums and the scatteredness *is* the practice, not destroying them or being upset or impatient with them. Understand that the mind is acting this way because it has lost its props; identify that as thinking, and relax. There is no need to respond. The mind will calm down when left alone.

Some people build up ego systems that say they are supposed to look good and have it all together. When the mind is seen in meditation, they realize they don't have it together and they don't want to see that. But a practitioner knows, without any shadow of a doubt, "I don't have it together. It is not my function in life to have it together. My function in life is to not be bothered by the thinking activity." That gives a tremendous amount of confidence, different from ordinary everyday confidence that is based on circumstances. You should have the confidence that no matter what state of mind comes up, no matter what situation comes up, you will be undisturbed. This is the gift of tranquility practice.

From time to time it is useful to reflect in moments where the fog clears. You should be able to reflect on, "I am now seeing into the emptiness of the ego structure." The truth of the Heart Sutra teachings will be revealed to your own mind: *all apparent beings are without a true self.* Realize that no matter what goes on in the body and mind, the illumination is unaffected in the same way that the sun is unaffected by clouds. Not even the thickest clouds, the tornadoes, and the hurricanes affect the shining of the sun.

If you know how to bring forth the sunshine of your being into everyday life through the simple practice of mindfulness and patience, then you have learned how to surf the mind, you have learned how to surf through life. This is the gift of practice. It is a gift that can be accomplished only with humility and tranquility. As you are walking, you should be able to bring forth the wisdom that the objects you are experiencing are one with your body—to hold, to catch that. And suddenly you and everything you are experiencing is recognized, understood anew.

If you want to understand the light that shines on the oneness of things, use the metaphor of dreaming. Suppose you have a dream that you are walking someplace. Where is the light that sees this dream taking place? Where is the location of that which sees it? If you understand this properly, you will perceive that the seeing of the dream is its existence—the taking place is the existence, there is not someplace from which you see it. The seeing of it is the entirety of the existence.

Try to catch that in this waking state too. The objects you are experiencing are ultimately not seen by a self that is located inside the body—that is empty. There is an astonishing mechanism inside the skin, but there is not an entity. The illumination of this world by consciousness is its existence. You and all things are being shone upon. In the same way the dreamer shines on the dream, you are being shined upon. This is where you find nirvana, this is God, this is the truth of being. The seat of existence is not inside the body. And when the body dies, there is nothing inside, no entity that passes away. We should know this.

Your death as a human being will be known by the same light that knows your life. Let your mind catch this point before it is too late. When you walk in the meditation line, contemplate that the objects that appear before your eyes are not seen by an ego that is behind the eyes. There is no "I" behind the eyes. The truth is that "I" is illuminating one world, one mind. This world is one entity that is empty of selves. If you have this kind of vision, you will walk through your life as if there is a light shining on you— because there is. Anytime you want to feel the light of God shining on you, all you have to do is release from "I am" in the thinking activity.

We take time to make the thinking activity irrelevant so that we can allow the deeper mind to experience the breathing. The thinking mind cannot experience breathing. The thinking mind can only experience thinking. The experience of the Buddha mind, of the deeper consciousness, is the entirety of this nondivided world.

I like to refresh the deeper elements of practice. Not just counting breaths—*one, two, three, four*—or getting lost in personal affairs during your zazen practice, but to realize that this God, divine consciousness, awareness, or Buddha mind is always with you. The mind cannot see it. The individual cannot know it. The individual mind subsides and basks in that sunshine, that is all.

7

The Great Goodness of Existence

WHEN WE ARE SITTING IN ZAZEN, what is the practice? It is to be aware that there are two simultaneous events taking place. There is the body sitting on the cushion, and there is the knowing that the body is sitting on the cushion. The body does not know it is actually sitting on the cushion. So if you know that you are sitting there, where does that knowing take place?

Most people, when sitting on the cushion, are just daydreaming or struggling somehow to escape from the psychological noise. But the act of knowing that one is sitting there is the great goodness of existence. The knowing that you are sitting there—or that you are walking or going to the bathroom—is miraculous. Unless you are texting—then you don't know that you are going to the bathroom. People don't value that they have the capacity to know what they are doing.

This knowingness may be referred to as the awareness or the Buddha mind. It can be seen as that element of our existence that is unborn and undying. It is always with us, but it is invisible until the inner eye opens. Start to appreciate the goodness of knowing and the goodness of existing—knowing and existing being the same function. It always has a quality to it of rock-solid sunshine. It is not something that can ever fail you or can ever not be there. Sometimes people go through experiences of being abandoned by a lover, by an old cat, by a relationship, or by a parent passing away. There is nothing else in the entire universe that is certain, except that wherever you are, you know that you are there. And that can always be relied upon. There is nothing that we can do as an individual that is as profound as knowing that we *are*. This knowing has been temporarily seduced and trapped in the thinking activity. It becomes visible when we are alive in the present moment, right where we are. That is when we will know it.

So, for example, if you woke up this morning and the sun was out and you saw it and you said, "*Ah*," that *Ah* is your basic goodness breaking through the thinking activity. Or maybe you are sitting in the zendo, and you hear a woodpecker banging or a crow cawing off in the distance, and suddenly you give yourself more to the sound than to your mental conversation. The moment sensation becomes more important than your mental conversation, the depth of the moment will contact you. And that depth is residing within you. It is not in the call of the crow, it is not in the woodpecker, it is not in the sunshine. It is our own sunshine breaking through the clouds—the clouds that are the obsession with personal life. The personal situation is always going to be pursuing the future. We are always going to be busy with something as an individual. You won't hear a crow because you don't get paid for it.

We were not born into life to suffer. We suffer because we have given the objective world authority over our emotional life—we have chosen to stress. I know that some people have children to raise and a career to take care of. And they may make the career very important, and the children may become an obstacle and a distraction from self-importance and self-fulfillment. Your child may say, "Why are you doing that?" Perhaps your dog says, "Why are you doing this?" And we do not have an answer except to push them away because the question is too painful. It is painful to feel the stress and the level of complication that life has become for many people.

When you come back to the meditation hall, there is always nothing new. You can count on practice because it is never different. Shoji comes over and offers you a cup of tea, and you take the teacup. And if you can't be present and thankful picking up the teacup, your practice is off. If you can't walk in a circle and put a smile on your face because finally there is nothing to be done, your practice is off. I hope you understand what a pleasant morning in the zendo consists of—that you are sitting here and you know that you are sitting here, and you know that nothing in your personal life can disturb that knowing. That knowing knows the disturbance, but the disturbance does not know the knowing. That is something that is with you forever and will never fail you.

8

When the Inner System is Broken

WE ARE WALKING TOGETHER on a "spiritual" path, using our intelligence and an honest examination of life as our guide. We can realize how we should live our lives—what it takes for us to be at ease, to be happy, to be free from fear and accept things as they are; to be able to enter into the mind and not be damaged, not to feel, "Oh, what a mess I am," or "I don't want ever to do this again." We want to be comfortable even in the presence of adversity.

To do this, we must cultivate a gentle spirit and abandon the neurotic ideas that society has embedded in us, one of the most damaging ideas being that when something hurts us, we should respond aggressively. This reactivity is deeply embedded in us. When our mind hurts, we don't usually think that it is our mind that hurts, we believe something external is hurting us, and we counter-attack. What is really happening is that our mind enters a painful state and blames it on outside circumstances. That is why, when we take up meditation practice, it is so important to acknowledge that we need to look at the situation with fresh, soft eyes. And this mood is most supported by acknowledging the temporary nature of our stay here.

The Ithaca Zen Center has an old brown van that is gradually dying, but we can't live without it, so we make believe that our brown van is eternal. Things are hanging off from underneath, the side panels are missing—and this is cracked and that is cracked. The human body is a similar thing. Our body, our ego, our trip in life, our career, our self-importance—these are all temporary affairs, these are not vehicles for fulfillment. These will also be lost.

This concept stands against the false cultural values that we are given, for we are raised in a world that says we are entitled to the pursuit of happiness. But we are not entitled to happiness, only the pursuit of happiness. People become enslaved to the pursuit of an experience that will complete them. "If I get that job, if I get this lover, if I get rich, I'll be happy forever." People who think that the pursuit of happiness is what life is about end up having to pray to something outside themselves because their inner system and their minds are broken. When the inner system is broken, you long for a savior, because you feel you are fundamentally incomplete.

But if you come to walk the spiritual path correctly, it will be precisely because you are broken, and you accept that you are broken, and you are embraced by your own acceptance. You are embraced by the fact that you can see the truth of your existence and you accept it. You smile about how neurotic it was to think you had to prove yourself worthy of existence by finding an unchangingly pleasant state.

To live, to be relaxed, to be happy should be the most natural things. But in the material world, people often need to be medicated in order to make it through. People need to have their minds anesthetized because the pressure that they put on themselves is unbearable. In meditation practice, take to heart the instructions about life. You don't attain anything in the meditation hall—the meditation hall is here to humble you, to free you from the stress and darkness that has accumulated in the mind. It humbles you by showing you where you are and where you could be.

When my teacher asked me to become a monk, I thought it meant to wear robes, be celibate, and shave my head. I was still in my twenties and I didn't want any of that. He said, "Okay, you don't have to do that." He said the saddest thing for him was to see a proud monk. "If anybody has ever done sesshin, how could they possibly be proud? How can you be proud of your psychological content? As a monk, that is not your job." It is the same now, whether or not you are a monk. You see what your mind is, and it may or may not be embarrassing, but it isn't anything you'd want to show to anyone. Well, maybe it *is* embarrassing. And this is the organ that the world is teaching you to be proud of. The thinking principle is a temporary activity that you have. It's like the brown van—it has a lifespan, and then it falls apart.

Taking pride in the thinking activity is the cause of suffering; laughing about the thinking activity is the cause of joy. That's all, it's that simple. Laughing about your life is simple. You were never meant to compete and succeed; you don't need a savior. You didn't go wrong, you just had a mistake placed inside you that says, *You will be loved and fulfilled by your accomplishments.* That poison was implanted there early on, from the first time your parents applauded when you went to the potty. Ever since then, there has been performance anxiety!

Life is an incredible gift you have been given. You are the natural evolution of a sperm and an egg that met and went through a will-less process that evolved into your current existence. We are the recipient of an incredible amount of grace to be able to exist, and we should appreciate that. And if you don't appreciate that your life is a miraculous gift, then you'll have to settle for the futile pursuit of happiness.

When the Muzak Stops

SOMETIMES WHEN WE RECEIVE an import like croissants or sushi, we think, *Oh very interesting, very exotic.* When we receive an import like Zen, we drink tea, wear robes, chant—it looks very exotic, very elegant, very spiritual. But please understand that the purpose of this practice is to free you from the activity of thinking, not to fascinate you, not for you to attain exotic spiritual states. Even though you may be wondering why you have to suffer through sitting here face to face with your mind—until you tire of your interest in yourself, that is how it will be. I'm sorry, that's what you have made of yourself.

When we have tea in the morning, it is just to calm us down, it is not an art form. It is easy to serve twenty people tea—nobody talks, very simple. And chanting is not to be saying anything of significance. Chanting is to remove you from the thinking activity. Sometimes when you are serving a nice meal, you have an hors d'oeuvre— and chanting is something like an hors d'oeuvre. You are going to have a main course, and it is going to be even less tasty—"I am going to do this horribly boring thing, so I'll do this somewhat boring thing before just to get in the mood."

Some people lack a correct understanding of what the mind is supposed to be doing in their life. That is why they suffer. People think that the proper use of the mind is to obtain pleasure and satisfactory states and to avoid uncomfortable experiences. But that is an incorrect use of the mind. If you lead a life based on deriving meaning from attainments and pleasures, you are going to run into situations that you will be unable to integrate. If that is what your life is about, things will happen that you will not be able to accept. In the natural course of events, we see that things go wrong all the time and people try to use the mind to fix them. Our teaching is that the great healer is boredom. We are expecting too much from our mind—it wasn't made to do what we are asking it to do. Because of that, the mind is overworked in the same way a muscle is overworked—it is straining. It is straining because it is heavily invested in a particular thought pattern called "like" and "don't like." Because the mind is for-ever sorting life into like and don't like, it is busy all the time. When you are doing zazen, you are putting yourself in a position to disable that function.

When experiencing your mental content in practice, you have the gentle but firm intention to maintain con-tact with the breathing activity. When you are sitting, when you are walking, you have the intention to experi-ence the breathing body. But in truth you cannot expe-rience the breathing, you can only allow the experience of breathing to take place. *You* cannot experience the breathing, because *you* are a thinking activity. If I say I am "David," that is a concept that I take myself to be. This "David" cannot experience the breathing, he is a word. If I want to experience breathing, "David" has to shut up. The same is true if you want to hug a friend or you want to feel the rain on your face. You cannot do that because the mind is so busy. But if the mind relaxes and stops, and you allow the awareness to contact the breathing, the rain will touch your face, and you'll go, *Ah!*

The mind does not stay fulfilled—it cannot. It makes a goal, and then it pursues this imaginary goal to be free of the pain of having a goal. If you establish a meditation practice, you can transcend that simply by experiencing your mental content without liking or disliking. This is something you can try to sort out with a therapist—or you can go inside honestly aware of your mental states. You are the most intimate with your own mind. And if you understand that the mind cannot be relied upon to solve its own issues, then you can relax. You are trying to allow the experience of breathing, and your mind is talking, talking, talking, and you don't care. You are not trying to fix your mind, you are just allowing it to unwind. In the course of allowing it to unwind, as you sit over a long period of time, there will be moments where the breathing experience breaks through the mental conversation.

The connection between the awareness and the breathing activity will always feel good. Your own natural state of being is always good. You are existing, and you may never have appreciated how good it is just to exist. This goodness will never desert you; you are never separate from the illumination of the awareness. Awareness will allow you to experience the cessation of the body. It may even feel, "Oh, so nice to get rid of that noisy thing—it hurts all the time."

You are always being shined upon by the illuminating consciousness, but you are not in contact with that because of the obsession of the thinking activity. So today is an all-day sitting, and if you are lucky, you will reach extremities of boredom. It is not that something wonderful happens. It is more like taking an elevator to the one hundred and tenth floor, where the Muzak version of a Beatles song is playing. The elevator is very slow, and you are listening to, "She loves you, yeah, yeah, yeah, she loves you, yeah, yeah, yeah," playing in the elevator over and over and over, when suddenly the Muzak stops. That is what happens in a day of sitting: Maybe the Muzak turns off; the incessant neurotic speed of the mind relaxes; and you find how beautiful is the sound of rain, how beautiful it is touching on the face—and the mind is quiet. These authentic experiences happen—experiences that in your personal life are valueless, but in the spiritual world are valued. What is authentic is the light that is allowing you to exist.

Please understand the practice correctly. Don't look for an answer to thinking or in thinking; just let it go, let it run like Muzak. To whatever extent you can, be there for the raindrops, be there for the breathing, be there for the eating. You will discover that when the mind is quiet, you are penetrated by goodness.

If you want to know how the teachings stay with you in everyday life, I can tell you for a fact that any moment that you stop you will experience the grace of God or the grace of your inner goodness, I guarantee. That is how it is, it is not some special thing. This is what the Buddha discovered; that there is within us an unborn, undying, illuminating essence. It is the Kingdom of Heaven.

10

Never Separate

TODAY IS MOTHER'S DAY, and a lot of people are spending the day with their mother saying thank you, or at least they are texting their mother to say thank you. When I first started questioning what my life should be about, and what direction I should go in, I lost my mother's love. My mother did not approve of the direction I was taking—from being an aspiring law student to that of being a good-for-nothing hippie. It was unbearable for her; she could not integrate that, and she ended up disinheriting me.

There is a Jewish custom that when a relative dies, you light a twenty-four-hour candle on the anniversary of their death to commemorate that person. My mother was so offended by my life that she started lighting a candle of mourning each year on my birthday. But she was also, in a certain way, no longer my mother—she was no longer a source of motherly love. I understood that the thinking mind, which was the seat of my personal existence, is like a dream. The thinking activity is a temporary thing like a body; identity as an individual is a temporary thing, but within it there is a truer, deeper self.

If you are attached to this body, believing it is the totality of your existence, when this body starts slowing down from old age, you will experience sorrow. It is sad that this thing that used to be so active and agile and vital is slowing down. But it is not tragic—now I don't have to waste my time doing things, I can just enjoy being here for as long as I can be here. People think that what is constant in their lives is this body. The mind is saying that what you are is this individuality, and that this body is your true identity.

This body is being experienced by something deeper than thinking. It is not different from us. It is not that it is somebody else, but that our original, true, unchanging existence is as consciousness. There is nothing constant in the body, there is nothing constant in the mind. But there is the constancy of the illumination of the body and the mind. I was fortunate to have a taste of that illumination; the true self beholds the individual, and that conscious- ness became my mother. I realized that I contained my mother, my mother is within me. And this mother's love never fails, it never accepts you then rejects you. No mat- ter how stupid your mind may appear, it never fails to let you know what you are thinking, it just shines on your mental content. The ego thinks, *I am this, I am that—I am everything I am doing.* But this *I am* doesn't really do anything but think.

When we are doing zazen, we are learning to align with our ultimate mother, with our true mother. And the way to do that is by humbly accepting and detaching from the mental content—to no longer be driven by what the mind is talking about, to no longer make life depen- dent on the thinking mind. Instead, our life is created by being grateful. We are not individuals tossed out into the world trying to fulfill ourselves. We are individuals tossed out into the world by the miracle of existence. And we are temporary forms, so we should make a vow. Even if the legs can't stand up, even if the body has become old and broken, when it is time to say goodbye, our posture is going to be, "I will let go, dissolve my appearance in this world, and simply come back home to the light itself that is unmanifested." Or perhaps, just come home to silence.

We do not have to do the grind of being an individual concerned about things—this is celebrating Mother's Day all the time. Within us is this element that will reveal itself when we release from the thinking activity —that's all. The thinking activity in which everyone is taking pride is the very thing which blocks the light that is beyond it.

My mother and I actually reconciled on her deathbed, seven years after she disinherited me. She died when I was twenty-nine years old. I sat next to her quietly. Everyone around her was miserable because, in the usual way of things, people consider death miserable. When someone is dying, people surround the dying person with their own fear and misery. I was spending time with her, saying very little, but being with her. And one morning she looked over to me and said, "You've been living in heaven these past few years, haven't you?" I started crying, and she started crying, and we had a very warm hug on her deathbed. And from then on out, we could only look at each other and smile, whereas others looked at her and were miserable.

Mother's Day is supposed to be a happy day. Please be glad that you will never be separated from your mother, your inner mother, which is your own deeper nature. Your mother is always with you as the illumination of your mind, that which is allowing you to behold the activities of thinking, seeing, hearing, smelling, tasting, touching. Never separate.

11

The Protection of the Dharma

WHEN THE FRAGILE SIDE OF LIFE shows itself, one's heart becomes more tender. When you are young and busy with your career, sometimes you miss the flowers, sometimes you miss the thunderstorm—life becomes about "me." When you sit in meditation practice, I hope that your practice is not based on becoming a good meditator. Meditation is fundamentally designed to calm you. When you come to Sunday morning services, be in the presence of the activity that creates your personal life, which is the thinking mind. Be with it and see what condition it is in, that's all. Then relax by not judging.

Many people do not have sufficient humility to experience the content of the mind without being embarrassed or not wanting to be there with it. And that is why meditation has traditionally been a monastic practice. I have heard that in countries with strong meditative traditions like Japan or South Korea, meditation is not practiced much by laypeople anymore. Laypeople go to ceremonies and support the monks, but often they don't practice meditation because it is difficult to go into meditation and not be discouraged.

It is only since coming to the West that the traditions of the monasteries have become part of the lay-community. The reason is that exposing people to the actual state of their minds may be unbearable. When you meditate, you are exposed to a more intimate experience of the mind. It requires a context that few people possess. We are not trained to experience the mind and remain unaffected by its content. Nevertheless, here we are, barbaric Westerners doing the monastic practices. And of course, it has tremendous blessings. Meditation gives you the experience that if you spend time in the awareness of breathing, your mental state will become clear. The chaos will settle and you will experience a relaxed inner condition that is always with you, but it is obscured by the stress factors introduced by the thinking activity. So, we come together for a couple of hours to endure the mental activity and then to witness its calming to whatever extent it happens. And of course, if you take any pride in the blessings, then you are back, lost in the thing that is tormenting you, so it is all wonderfully ironic anyway.

Last week in the zendo a tremendous dizziness came over me, to the point of my just about falling over. The Jiki carried me halfway down, and I ended up in the hospital. Doctors were trying to figure out if something serious was happening or not. Fortunately, I had no idea about much except that there seemed to be some level of concern. The next morning, it was over. But in the context of it, there was a lovely feeling of having the protection of the dharma. Wherever you go, you have the protection of what you have been cultivating in your practice—nonreaction to circumstances and nonreaction to mental states. I hope you can have a sense of what this practice is offering you—to be inert and amused simultaneously.

When you are practicing breathing awareness, even though there is the psychological chop suey going on, there is also the experience of the breathing, to whatever extent it is noticed. This experiencing of the breathing is monumentally significant. It means that you are witnessing the very identity that you consider yourself to be. You are experiencing a level of detachment from the identity that the mind is asserting as the only identity that you have. If the only identity that you have is the thinking activity, and thinking activity starts to go mumbo jumbo, you will be frightened. If you want to know why you experience fear, it is because the temporary identity that you have assumed is being threatened, your very existence is being threatened. The thinking activity is unable to integrate whatever it is.

I know there are some people who practice here and try to work really hard in their meditation practice, but that does not always work. The thinking activity does not witness the breathing even though it says it does. It says, *I am breathing,* but it isn't. It is thinking, it is not breathing. Breathing is breathing. So, when Buddha gave the fundamental teaching that says, "Breathing in, I am aware of breathing in, breathing out, I am aware of breathing out," that "I" is the Buddha mind. There is this element within us that is deeper than the thinking activity. Little by little we chip away at what prevents us from knowing this.

Also, I want to mention that bowing at the end of practice is not a yoga exercise. When you are bowing at the end of practice, you are manifesting self-negation with your body. You are doing your best to manifest that your body is not your true nature. People who think the way to fulfill oneself is through the glory of this body, to ornament it with tattoos and jewelry and fancy clothes, are making a dangerous mistake. The extent to which this body is glorified as the totality of identity is the depth to which you will experience the fear of its demise. We are putting the body down to the floor to say, "This is my path, it is not the enhancement of self. My path is the release from self, the dissolution of self."

In the end, you will see that this body and this universe was one body with no self in it from the beginning. The whole idea that you live in an objective world that has nothing to do with you is a mistake of the thinking mind. The entire notion that this universe is separate from you is a mistake of the thinking mind. And the sooner that mistake is corrected, the sooner you won't have to sit zazen.

12

A Flawed Agenda

MOST OF US have been fed a certain understanding of the direction of our life, and what constitutes success and failure. We have a basic cultural agenda, which few people question. It is only when the agenda fails that we take a deeper look at things. What people don't realize, of course, is that the agenda always fails.

Once I went to chelation treatment, and there was a woman next to me who had an untreatable disease. She had lived a very healthy life and had tried every kind of treatment, and something was supposed to work, but nothing worked, and she was outraged that she only had a couple of months left to live. It did not fit with her understanding of how life should be, and she was ready to take up arms against God. Obviously, she thought, God was unjust to do something like that to her. This is how the mind works when its fundamental approach to things is frustrated. It is very fortunate when we can actually hear the noble truth as taught by a wise being who looked deeply into it. People usually do not hear the noble truth. It is called noble because it tells a painful truth. This is the noble truth: Life is suffering, it is not an agenda for success.

The Buddha dared to go against the stream to honor a teaching like this. He didn't say, "God will save you," and he didn't say, "At the end of your life you will go to heaven." He said that your agenda is innately broken, that the plan you have for your life is flawed, and you are going to suffer because you have a flawed agenda. It's not good or bad, that's just how it is. Some people take a while to learn that. This woman in the chelation room hadn't learned it. When I spoke to her, I said, "Do you really want to depart in that state of mind?" She replied, "With my last ounce of strength I will curse God." So even in this little room, there was a drama of biblical proportions!

The reason the agenda fails is because the thinking activity is impermanent. It does not last forever, and it has no stable core, no self in it. The thinking activity contains the entirety of personal life. Your existence as an individual is a content of the thinking activity; it takes place in that part of the mind, and that part of the mind that thinks has to be supported by a structure called the brain, and that is a temporary thing.

Even Einstein's brain, though preserved in formaldehyde in a museum, doesn't do much thinking anymore. Same for us. If our thinking is based on fulfilling ourselves as individuals, then it is flawed, because as individuals we cannot be fulfilled by something that is going to disappear. Why is it that people get all stressed out? Because they are trying to fulfill something that is imaginary by chasing after ideas like "I have to do this, I have to do that" until their minds are tied in knots. They do not see the flaw in what they are doing, they do not realize they are using an imaginary entity to find what the purpose of their lives is and what will fulfill them.

Another noble truth is that suffering has a cause that can be realized. There is a way to realize what it is within us that is beyond the thinking activity, and upon which a life based on the impermanence of the ego can be lived. That life is based on treating others as yourself so that you deemphasize your individuality. It is not based on attaining as an individual, but rather on lovingkindness. The notion that the self is living inside this body is the flawed agenda. The true self—the actual self, not a self that is created by the thinking activity, but that actually is—is illuminating us.

In religious terms, God, or the consciousness, is illuminating our existence but, fundamentally, it is not born into our personal existence. In the same way, the sun is shining on us but is not within us. Just now everybody is very excited about eclipses. People like exciting experiences: *The sun is going to disappear*! In the old days, there was an idea that a dragon or a demon in the sky was eating the sun and if we didn't pray, the sun might be eaten. Nowadays people think, "I want to see the eclipse," and when the eclipse has passed, "Well, what was that all about?"

You won't let us enjoy anything!

That is precisely the point. There is no need to enjoy anything in particular when you can enjoy everything. When you don't enjoy anything, you enjoy everything: "I'm so happy during every solar eclipse." The fact that the sun is shining all the rest of the time, and the moon and the stars—well, what's the point? But an eclipse, *whoa!* That has a corollary to it. The point is that the pure enjoyment of yourself is so authentic and beautiful that anything that satisfies you as an individual is alright, but of no lasting significance.

In zazen practice, it can be years before you really understand that your body is a vessel that you are experiencing. It takes a long time to see this, but this is what you are trying to awaken to. The thinking activity proclaims that the body is the identity. Please understand that your identity as a body, this individuality that you are taking yourself to be, is only that because of the thinking activity saying, "I am living inside this body, and therefore I should fulfill myself through my success story because this is what I am." The thinking activity is just a dream, there is no entity living inside this structure. This is the teaching of the Heart Sutra, this is the teaching of the awakened ones—that in truth you are the divine light. Your identity is not as a thing, it is the sunshine of consciousness. When you do zazen, all you are doing is putting your body in a position and looking at it until you realize, "I" is the one who beholds it. This is the path of awakening to the true transpersonal self or the true nature of being.

I say these words to encourage you to try to see it clearly. There is no shortcut to this insight, you really have to cross the stream of thinking without getting caught in it. It takes some time to realize that you are the one *watching* the thought process, you are not the one *in* the thought process. But maybe one day when you are walking down the road, and you become aware of your body walking down the road, and you feel a quietness come over you, and a smile comes on your face, you will realize God is with you. Every moment of your life, God is illuminating your existence. Then you will not need an agenda, you will have found that which is beyond all agendas—much better than seeing an eclipse.

13

Signing on to Suffering

PEOPLE ARE ACCUSTOMED to religion having to do with higher powers. Why do people get involved in religion? They want to feel connected to something deeper in life than the everyday grind. They look for something that will lift them up by imagining that there is some heaven; that there are some saints, messiahs, prophets; that there is an almighty being in the sky who is manipulating human affairs and will come to their aid. It rarely occurs to people to examine the nature of the mind itself to solve the human condition.

I hope you don't think of Buddhism as a religion. Buddhism is an instruction manual on the nature of the mind and how it can become free of suffering. Fundamentally, it is the mind's tendency to react aggressively against what bothers it that needs to be identified as the enemy. If we allow the mind to create an enemy and allow the mind to attack it, and blame our problem on the enemy, it is impossible to find peace.

Perhaps, if you are in an academic environment, you are being taught that the way to live your life is to outdo others. That is how you prove your self-worth. Your value is built on outperforming others. What becomes of your relationship to human beings when you are living in that kind of situation? Your relationship to human beings is perverted and competitive, your relationship to work is stressful because your performance, hence your self-worth, is on the line all the time. People take on huge stress factors and ignore what that does to the quality of their lives. All of this in the pursuit of happiness. Even professors live under pressure: to publish or perish. I only mention this because Ithaca has several academic penitentiaries in it, so a lot of the inmates come here for visitation hours.

Please understand what you are doing. It is painful to see people signing on to suffering, signing on to stressful lives, signing on to situations where it becomes impossible to enjoy going for a walk or seeing a flower. Those small moments are seen as useless aberrations because they are not furthering the personal situation. It's very serious, and our whole culture is like that. The thing to take care of is your mind, along with the situations of your life. The situations of your life are secondary. You have to deal with them, but you'd be amazed how much easier it is to deal with life when you don't feel your self-worth is on the line. Life is not about achievement, life is about acknowledging that your stay here is impermanent, so flow softly and gracefully. Once you realize that no matter what you do your existence is a temporary appearance, you'll see that putting yourself into a pressure situation to achieve and to be in competition with others is neurotic and creates the consequences of unpleasant mental states. With this realization, your life changes.

When you sit in meditation practice, you get the week in review. You get to look at how your mind behaved by simply seeing what is in it. Your awareness goes toward the breathing, and that allows the mind to be free to roam. And you will see what its contents are and whether it is doing ridiculous things like judging itself. The mind's judging itself is one of the most fruitless things it can do. You have the opportunity to see that the mind is occasionally neurotic and that the quality of your life is enhanced by just allowing it to relax and be content. That is the fulfillment of life: when you acknowledge the situation is impermanent, that all of your achievements will turn into thin air, and that there is nothing permanent you can create. At the same time, acknowledge that being alive is a gift, not something that you have done on your own.

For the mind to have the capacity to think, it has one of the most sophisticated structures on the planet as its basis. This body—with its billions of interdependent neurons, organs, and systems—operates without a will. There is no will needed for the body to know how to warm itself, or how to excrete, or how to sweat, or how to walk. You don't have to do that with the will; the body functions to support its own life. And one of the things it supports is thinking. You have all these interconnecting systems operating to enable you to think. Do you ever think that if a few things went wrong, thinking would disappear? Your system could not support it.

The thinking activity is insanely arrogant. It says, *I exist independent of the body*. When you are walking in meditation practice out in the woods, is your mind walking with you, or is your mind off someplace else thinking this, thinking that? It is very rarely with you; it goes off by itself and creates neurotic moment after neurotic moment. The practice is to bring the mind back to the body or to allow the awareness to experience breathing. If you can experience your body, it means your mind is relaxed. It is that simple, it is not an esoteric thing.

Your mind is relaxed, it's clear, it's lucid. It's allowing the awareness to see the basic situation—this is the practice. This can actually be cultivated; you can restore sanity to your operating system, you can remove stress if you just look closely and use common sense.

14

A Guide For Your Mind

ONE OF THE MAJOR DIFFERENCES between spiritual and religious ideas is whether the highest principle is contained within us or whether it exists as an objective experience outside of us. Our understanding is that the principle exists within us but is simply obscured by the thinking activity. Consequently, we don't experience the illumination within us, we experience the thinking activity. Meditation practice is taking the voyage from this shore to the other shore, taking a voyage through the thinking activity into tranquility and insight. In tranquility, there is natural ease, and in insight, an undisturbed, noble illumination, which is with us from the beginning.

Cultivate patience as you cross through the thinking activity. Most people know the experience of inner goodness because it is not remote from us. Some morning you might be walking along, notice the sunrise, notice that the air has a fresh quality to it, and stop for the sunrise. *Ah!* Then you feel that there is something extraordinarily good about the whole thing. The sun rises, there are pink skies—who bothered to do that? What a fine, considerate thing! You feel the presence that is revealed by the mind stopping. In the quiet of the mind appreciating the morning, we experience *Ah!*

Eventually, this gets covered over and disappears. People recognize this and want to preserve it with a picture. When we see a sunrise, the first thing we do is whip out our cell phones. We think that goodness and beauty are located in the sunrise. "I'll take a picture of this, and I will capture the goodness and the beauty." But the goodness and the beauty are arising within you. You stop, the thinking stops, and then you experience this feeling of *Ah!* So next time you want to take a picture of the sunrise, just turn around and take a picture of yourself and say, "Oh, here I am, beautiful and quiet." Forget about the sunrise picture.

We have been taught from a young age to be important, and the burden of having to prove ourselves destroys us. At the moment we have a wonderful example of a pregnant female body in the meditation hall. What is really happening is an entirely natural activity with no self-will. You don't do anything for this to happen, this baby is produced by a chain of causation. You can say it goes back to a sperm and an egg, but if you really look at it, the sperm comes from preconditions, the egg comes from preconditions, and they come together. This thing that is going on inside—the growth of a fetus—the "I" really has nothing to do with it. It is just being done. Are the baby's body and mother's body separate? Are there two entities? At what point does the baby become an entity? In Buddhism we might say there is no "I" in the structure; it is composed of form, sensations, perceptions, thinking, and consciousness. It grows like an apple tree, and at some point it manifests.

When a mother has the experience of seeing her baby, it is a powerful moment. The experience is that a part of myself is now visible to me, this is my own self appearing to me. That experience produces great love. That spiritual experience is similar to the meditative insight that comes to a practitioner. You realize that the objects of the senses, which are the entire universe, are one with this body. The sky is the part of this body called *eyes*— everything that you relate to is part of your body. A fundamental teaching is that there is no experience that is not produced by the physical body. The whole universe is produced by the physical body. That is the glory of your existence—not that you earn this much money or that you accomplish this and that. That is trivial compared to experiencing "My body is one with the whole universe."

We don't realize we are producing the whole universe; we see the world as being objective. But it has been born out of our body, the same way a baby is born out of the mother's body. When a practitioner is walking around in this human life and not absorbed in the thinking activity, that practitioner can realize that this universe and ourselves are both arising. We arise simultaneously together and are now seeing this universe as our "other half."

This universe is functioning as a set of conditions, and just as a human being is subject to birth and death, whole worlds are subject to birth and death. The structure of things is to have forms and egos appear. And egos—selves that function under the idea that they are separate from the universe—tend to destroy things for their own self-interest. I would suggest to you that, even if this wisdom does not awaken in you for some time, you use it as a guide for your mind. In some religions, you are told that somebody appeared as a god. In this situation, you are being told that you are appearing as one with the universe and that you should treat the universe kindly—that inside every being is your self. The same illumination that is your source is illuminating within every being. There is only one mind existing, but this mind appears to lose contact with itself, goes astray. Live your life as if you are living inside every creature and you will never make a mistake. To the extent that you know that that which is awake within you is within everybody else, you will spontaneously feel kindness for the suffering of yourself inside another being.

We produce suffering by identifying ourselves as a self that is separate from everything. In this tradition, that is called the source of suffering. Whereas if what you want is the happiness of others, then your thinking is in accordance with the deeper reality. If you take the happiness of others to be your happiness, then you will have your own religious contract; you will have a connection to your own salvation, your own freedom from worry about life and death and pleasure and pain. These will be seen to be thinking based on the "I" being separate. And this is the kind of heart that wisdom produces; that inside, everyone is the same, and that the universe as it is appearing is one with you.

15

Skywriting in the Mindspace

WHAT IS IT THAT ZEN TEACHERS are trying to explain? They have seen into the structure of the mind and have noticed that people suffer from having mistaken ideas about the nature of that mind. They have seen that all beings are structured the same way, but those who are blind to this become emotionally invested in themselves and suffer from ignoring the noble truth of impermanence, and the insight that there is no "I"—no true self—in the body-mind matrix. The true self is transcendent.

Because of this misunderstanding, people spend their lives trying to accomplish and prove themselves as individuals without understanding how it is that their individuality arises, how it is that they are existing. It may take a long time for the thinking mind to become humble. It has been trained to be arrogant. We were raised that we exist separate from all other creatures, that we as individuals are self-existing.

Based on self-existence, people are trying to satisfy themselves to the best of their abilities. But when you meet the wisdom teachings and have the experience that the personal self is impermanent, that everything you do is going to disappear, it is like running into a concrete wall. Everything in which you are intellectually and emotionally invested becomes viscerally seen to be that which is producing the fear of dying, and the inability to find stable happiness.

If the thinking mind identifies itself as an ultimate true identity, this may become tragic. Terrible things can happen. You can become serious; you are in danger of taking yourself seriously, instead of being like a little child playing in the Kingdom of Heaven. You become someone with serious problems. Sometimes these problems become so hardened that they get names and become rock solid. People cannot find a way out. There are people who practice who have received many times the teaching that says, "Do not react emotionally to your psychological content." As an expression of the depth of insight, the usual response is, "I can't believe how crazy I have been."

What people are not seeing is that a mind based on the identification of its own self-existence is itself tragic; it is not that they are doing something wrong. How can people possibly make sense of life if they really consider its impermanence? How does one let the mind assert these things without reflecting, "Wait a second, what is this?"

The heart of this practice is to awaken from the mental conversation that you are mistakenly calling your true self. You awaken to the truth that the true self is the detached illumination of that conversation; this is called mindfulness practice. It takes mindfulness to awaken you from the hypnosis of the mental conversation. It is not just during sitting practice that your existence is spiritual, your existence should be spiritualized all the time. "Spiritualized" means nonaggressive and grateful. Don't buy into a line of logic that produces stress.

The deeper nature of consciousness is never stressed, it is always calm. But it experiences the activity of the mind being stressed, saying, "I'm stressed, I have so much to do." The contact with the original illumination is obscured. If you can see through that in meditation practice or in everyday life, if you can create a moment which is not dominated by thinking, if you can just walk in meditation and feel the body walking, you will realize that you are the experiencer of the body. You cannot realize that until the mental conversation calms down.

My mother was Orthodox Jewish. The religious usually carry with them a large load of ideas about the nature of God and ethics. She was angry at me because I left the religion. So she disinherited me and did not want to see me for seven years. But when she was dying and knew she was dying, we fell in love with each other again. The pointlessness of her reaction to my life became apparent to her. "What's the point? I'm leaving here and look what I created."

At the end of my mother's days, it was just relaxing and disappearing. All those things that had bothered her for seven years just disappeared. That is how it's going to be for everyone at some point. When we see how fragile, how precious, how miraculous it is that we are existing, then all self-concerns will look foolish. People who are trying to prove importance or gain wealth, or who try to make these the goals of their lives, will always be neurotic. They will never stop.

Zen practice may be said to be the worship of the mind stopping. It *is* the worship of the stopping mind, it is the worship of peace of mind. When the mind calms down, what is your experience? If you want to experience this worshipful state, where does your mind go? Where does your mind go when you are breathing in? Where does your mind go when you are walking? Where does your mind go when you are breathing out? Where does your mind go when you are drinking a cup of tea? It becomes lucid. And what you are doing becomes tender and present. Drinking a cup of tea with nothing else to do, just this moment. Walking on the Earth, just this moment. You experience the lucidity of the present moment. In the lucidity of the present moment, you realize that your deeper nature is shining on this body you have been calling yourself.

If that experience becomes deeper, you realize that the true nature is never born and never dies. What dies is the thinking activity, which is not a true self. It is just skywriting in the mind space. All the wisdom of every spiritual tradition enters into you. You experience what the founders of every religion experienced: that there is a deeper living essence, and that your existence as an individual is a temporary activity of consciousness and has no intrinsic significance. The significance of your existence is for you to realize the illuminating nature of the original source that you have appeared from. Every creature is in the same situation. There is no such thing as, "I am an individual"—that is a creation of the thinking activity.

These are what are called the *prajna* teachings. These are the wisdom teachings, which are the basis of spiritual life. These teachings are not based on a messiah or on worshipping something that happened in the ancient past. They are based on the truth about the nature of reality. That which is called "I" is not contained within you. This is called, in the Heart Sutra, "Saved from all suffering and distress"; it is the end of psychological suffering. Then you will experience only the physical suffering of sitting zazen! You don't have to worry; you don't need to have performance anxiety. Can you imagine waking up in the morning with no pressure whatsoever? Your only job when you wake up in the morning is to brush your teeth and to realize that you are alive and gifted another day—that you are no longer in the evaluated, judged world. You have been freed from that by your own intelligence. What could be more glorious?

This wisdom is not something outside you, so whether you are here or there or anywhere, this is your structure. Whether you are in California, in Florida, at the North Pole, at the South Pole, the structure of your consciousness and your existence is always the same. There is a thinking activity, and there is the fundamental illumination of that which is always smiling on you, called the golden sunshine of your true nature. If you live a life based on this understanding, the insight will develop over time. Things that bothered you will no longer bother you. The doubts that you have about self-fulfillment may be seen as comical.

Someone at sesshin came into an interview and said to me, "I have to make this incredibly important decision, and I want to know how I can use practice to make the right decision." That is usually a question that someone gets paid three hundred dollars an hour to answer, not something you ask in some free interview. I said to her, "Before you tell me what this question is, here is the answer: No matter what you choose, it's wrong. Okay, now make your choice."

That is what happens when you don't pay for advice! That's how it is. There is a scripture that talks about a log floating down a river. When it encounters an island in the middle of the river, the log starts stressing out, "Should I go to the left or to the right?" And it is thinking, going "Left, right, what should I do, what should I do?" Meanwhile, the river just takes it downstream. The log is going down the right side of the island, thinking, "Should I have gone on the left side of the island?" That is what a human mind does.

I hope this becomes something that saturates you as the weeks and months and years go by, so that as you mature, your practice matures and your spirituality deepens. Your spirituality deepening means that you know no external event can satisfy you. The belief that external events will produce satisfaction fades.

Even if you have the idea that the mind has been damaged because you had traumatic experiences at some point, this is not the case. This is the mind trying to perpetuate itself. Have the courage to come from the dharma wisdom. Have the courage to take a serious and sincere look at what you are doing with your life. Have the courage to go against the stream of self-importance. Have the courage to see into the inevitability of your own passing away. It is pointless to worry about things. When the true nature of things is put in your face, you just say, "Thank you very much, things are much easier."

If you see these things clearly through, you enter the goodness of being alive. You are reconnected to the goodness of pure existence. People are often unconscious of the goodness of having ears. We forget that it is miraculous that we can hear, see, smell, or touch; that the body has such a complex operating system and that it does these ten billion functions so that consciousness can have a home.

Your body allows consciousness to be born, but your body is not your true self. Your body is this astonishing vehicle that has evolved. You are the god born into this body seeking itself. But the mind is saying, "No, you are not the god; I am the god. This body is the true existence." If the mind says it is the true existence, it cannot appreciate the miracle of eyes, ears, nose, and tongue. It cannot experience it, but you can, if you free yourself from delusion.

There is a lovely student who made an enormous leap out of normalcy and ended up banging his head a little bit. When you leap out of worldly normalcy into spiritual normalcy and wake up with your banged head, you may think, "How do I put all this together? Which way do I go? What do I do?" When you see the comedy of that mental conversation, it will give you enough to laugh about for a month.

When a community practices together, there is a natural warmth that the dharma produces. And that warmth gathers the sangha. It gathers people who acknowledge that they are broken. It is very different from the convention of a political party, where people gather together to win, to defeat the enemy. No, the dharma makes you understand that egotism is the enemy. Aggressive, self-based mind has been destroying your life for as long as you know. And then you hear something that says, "No, this isn't the way." People can look at each other and smile and feel a connectedness because we are all the same consciousness incarnated in different forms. Once we say, "I am this form," then everybody is different from you.

This is the only way that existence can happen. We all come down, spend a few years as arrogant imbeciles, and then meet something that says, "Do you know you are an arrogant imbecile?" And you just say, "Oh, thank you very much, I feel better now."

That is the warmth of a sangha. Whether you are CEO of a corporation or a garbage collector, whether you are an opera singer or a dishwasher, you are united because you can look inside and see yourself. You do not see people different from you, you start seeing that people are your true self appearing. If you cannot handle people right away, because many people are not living in that world, then try a poodle if you want to see what it looks like for the light to look back at you with open eyes.

16

The Mistaken Seat
of Consciousness

ZEN PRACTICE can seem to have a stark, cold feel to it. The chanting is not exactly operatic, and the sitting is without television. Even though it has a bare quality, that is only on the outside. In the real practice the body is cool and the heart is warm—this is the feeling of the practice.

So chanting can feel very dull, and if you try to produce a warmth out of it, you can't do it—it just becomes tight. Real chanting comes from being relaxed, and if you are sitting there relaxed, you are going to produce a warm sound from a warm heart. How do you produce a warm heart when you are chanting? The warmth of your heart appears as the intimacy of the consciousness and the vocal cords. The intimacy of it—so that when you are chanting, the fullness of being contacts the vocal cords. That intimacy is the warmth of your heart. The consciousness inside is always warm. The vocal cords are flesh and blood—the vocal cords have no self. If you examine your vocal cords, you cannot find anybody there. You cannot say, "*I am chanting*," because chanting is the activity of the vocal cords. The contact of the consciousness with the vocal cords allows you to experience this intimacy. In the intimacy of the consciousness with the vocal cords, a great miracle happens. The miracle is that the mind becomes aware that the consciousness exists as the witness.

Becoming aware of your deeper existence through this intimate contact with the physical body is basically what mindfulness practice is. When you are walking, it is not just an exercise of walking, you are actually experiencing your feet and your body. You cannot produce intimacy—it is a preexisting condition. When you experience breathing, what exactly do you have to do to have that experience? To experience birds singing, to experience vocal cords talking, to see snowflakes or trees? What activity do you perform to do that? There is no need to do anything. But you need to let go of the self that resides in thinking.

If you are thinking, you will not be able to hear a bird. It may take two to three days of sitting in a retreat before you can hear a bird sing and become one with the bird. Human beings do not realize that we are in an inaccurate and fallen state. Fallen does not mean good or bad, it just means confused. The consciousness is obscured by the thinking activity. It does not realize that it has descended into the thinking activity. As individuals, we say this is what we are; we do not realize that it is the mental conversation, not a true self, that is creating our life. We do not realize that the thinking activity is an impermanent activity. You will not be able to think forever, thank God. Dying is a problem only for the misconceived self. My teacher used to say he enjoyed performing funerals but did not enjoy performing weddings. The reason he enjoyed performing funerals was that no one has ever complained about their funeral service, and no one has ever not complained about their wedding!

If you can see the structure, you can see the human condition. Buddhist teaching is the calling out to those who dwell unquestioningly in the human condition. It is the compassionate response to seeing people suffering in a vain attempt to find happiness as an individual. The sadness of the fallen human state is its attempt to find happiness and meaning in an impermanent situation. And so it offers this teaching of intimacy or love, if you prefer, or penetrating awareness. If you allow the consciousness to intimately experience the body in a clear and full way, the mind awakens to the truth—that the true self is the pure consciousness rather than the body or ego. The self is not contained within the breathing activity, it illuminates the breathing activity. And in the intimacy of that experience, awakening happens—the mind awakens from the identity that has been mistakenly imposed on it by the thinking activity. It knows, "I am originally existing and illuminating prior to the thinking activity, I am the illumination." It all comes from moment-to-moment mindfulness, which is impossible to maintain when the identity is fixated in thinking.

So, when the thoughts come—"I can't live without him, I can't live without her, how will I pay my taxes, how will I live my life, what should I do"—we do not realize that we are sitting in an insatiable condition. The thinking activity can never find an answer that says, "Okay, all finished, now I am complete." If we understand the human condition properly, we will understand that when we identify as an individual we are sitting in an insatiable condition. Knowing and accepting that insatiable condition is called the end of suffering. It is the end of a life plan called "Fulfilling yourself through external circumstances." That strategy is broken, and the abandoning of that strategy is called wisdom.

To further explain this mistaken seat of consciousness, I would like to say a word or two about dreaming. When you dream, from what point do you see your dream? Imagine you are walking on the beach. There are waves, seagulls, pelicans. From where do you see the dream? The mind creates this whole scene. From where does it see that scene?

The point from which your life is ultimately being seen is not within this body. It's the same as when you dream that you are walking on the beach: You are not seeing the beach from within the body that is walking on the beach. The body that is walking on the beach is a psychological creation. In the same way, during ordinary waking experience, your personal life is a psychological creation. In truth, this universe is illuminating as oneness. This whole universe is the "body" of one mind. And to take up the identity of an individual—within this universe or within a dream—is a fallen state. "Fallen state" means that the identity, the self, is not being seen as it truly is. Existence is being seen through a dirty window, so to speak, through the lens of a mind that says, "I am an individual." It is identical to the way one might be walking on the beach in a dream through the idea in the mind that has accepted as its identity being an individual walking on the beach. The truth is that the mind is appearing as the oneness of the scene.

The mind essence is bringing the totality into existence, and then falls into its dream the same way it falls into a human identity. The pathway out is to awaken from that and the way to do so is to love thy neighbor as thyself, or to see this whole universe as one with you, even though you are now living as an individual. You are born and connected to the whole the same way the person in a dream walking on the beach is connected to the sand, and the wave, and the pelicans. It is one flashing of the consciousness.

When you are chanting, first you have to learn the words, then you relax. You relax your voice, and you can tell when your voice is relaxed if it comes into your chest instead of being stuck in a tightness of the throat. You are beholding chanting, observing the contact of the consciousness with the vocal cords. You are experiencing chanting the praise of that which is beholding. That is a beautiful experience; the mother and the child are one. The consciousness illuminates the body, and the body praises the illumination.

17

Completion Comes
from Gentleness

N ZAZEN ONE BECOMES more keenly aware of the content of the mind. Most people do not realize they *have* a mind. Most people think they *are* the mind. If you think you are the mind, then it is difficult to work on the mind, because it is difficult to find the place from which to work on it. The thought content will be taken personally.

This thing that is talking within us determines the quality of our life. We are rarely taught to cultivate it—to cultivate happy mental states, gentle mental states, stress-free mental states. We are taught to use the mind to advance our personal situation in the world, and that idea is the work of the devil. It is the devil because it puts us in hell. The idea that we are going to fulfill ourselves as individuals is the gateway to hell, because we cannot fulfill something that is impermanent.

Sometimes when I sit with people, I take on the flavor of their background. Knowing that there are Catholics in the meditation hall, I end up talking about the Bible. And knowing that there are musicians in the meditation hall, I end up talking about the crow crying out during zazen. Musicians may think, "When I hear the bird, I know that I am quiet enough to hear the bird. Usually, I'm too busy.

When I heard the bird, it's not just that I hear the bird, it's a sign that my mind is lucid. It's not so busy that I can't even hear a bird." That's the Bird Bible: "This is how to live. This is how your mind should function."

Once you think you are going to fulfill yourself as an individual, you lose contact with appreciating that you exist. You lose contact with what a miracle it is to be. You get thrown out of the Garden of Eden and open the gateway to Hell. When sitting in zazen, you are cultivating a relationship to the thinking activity by being aware of it and accepting it as it is. You are not trying to suppress it; you are not trying to do anything other than allow it to flow. That is called *water meditation* in the sutras. Let the mind flow like a stream, and it will find its own peace.

Everyday life is very different. The mind is needed to decide how we are going to pay our student loans, our mind is needed to decide whether we are going to Walmart or Target. The mind is needed to do these things, and we cannot just observe it, because we are in it. We cannot just experience it in a detached mood. Nowadays, instead of letting the mind relax, when people have a free moment they play with some technology and do not sink back into themselves. Without sinking back into yourself, you lose track of the fundamental miracle of your existence. You do not appreciate just waking up in the morning. People misuse their minds badly; they get down on themselves, which is one of the strangest things one can do. We divide ourselves into two parts, and one belittles the other. No one explains to you how pointless that is. When you judge yourself, when you get down on yourself, it is no different than using your right hand to punch your left arm.

The mind is dividing itself into two parts—one acting and one judging. And the judge can be pretty severe. Your mind is malfunctioning, and instead of thinking, "Oh, my mind is malfunctioning, I should allow it to relax," people take a drug or engage in some activity so they can get rid of this tension. Spirituality is cultivating the wisdom of caring for the mind. And if you cannot be forgiving and kind to yourself, you will never be able to forgive anyone else. If you find something in yourself that is unforgivable, how can you forgive that same quality when it shows up in someone else? Impossible. And you will never be truly able to love someone unless you can love yourself.

If you cannot have a sense of humor about what a fool you are, then you are misusing your mind in such a way that it produces suffering. That is why a monk said, "The meek shall inherit the Earth." You should cultivate meekness. To be meek, to have a humble feeling about yourself, is more precious than a BMW and it will bring you more happiness than having a Tesla. To be a peacemaker, to be able to make peace with being yourself, will bring you more happiness than winning a lottery.

To hear a bird and appreciate that you have an organ that can perform this activity gives you greater wealth than trying to find something external to make you happy. If you suddenly discovered that you had millions of dollars left to you by a great uncle, what would you do with that money? Would you try to buy yourself happiness? We might have the thought, "Now I can do everything that I always wanted to do. I can do all the neurotic things that I couldn't do before," and then start chasing around like a gerbil on a rotating wheel. Zazen is different—it teaches you that you should learn how to relax and be with this mind you are experiencing. And your life as it is should be relaxed.

Maybe you are jealous of Jeff Bezos. He is the richest man in the world, which means he can get anything he wants at Amazon. But usually, when you can get anything you want at Amazon, it is difficult to be happy about a muffin or about a bird song. There is not necessarily any connection between happiness and wealth. It is good to have enough money to be able to feed yourself, but there is no proving self-worth. You do not attain some level where you say, "I have done this, and now I am complete." No, you will never have that experience except for a passing moment. Your completion comes from your gentleness.

When you are doing zazen, you are slowly extricating your consciousness from neurotic mental activity. When you take your seat, your body should be relaxed and comfortable, your mood should be relaxed. Have no resistance to anything that comes up in the mind. No desire to chase away negative thoughts, no desire to push them away. There is no desire to bring in exquisite, beautiful things. Just be indifferent. And in that indifference, you are finding the peace that surpasses all understanding. Born out of that peace, you appear in this world as kindness. This is the true spiritual path, this is what real religion should be—not belief in external gods, or angels. It is the humbling of the heart, allowing the natural lovingkindness and gratitude that is in it to come forth. That should be your religion.

What's Next?

'D LIKE TO SAY A FEW WORDS about the fundamental understanding of the spiritual path and the meditation practice. Some of you have been practicing for a while and probably have heard this several times already, but it bears repeating and is also an introduction to the profoundness of the meditative insight and the spiritual way of life.

When you are doing anything in life, there are always two of you, so to speak. There is the one who thinks, "I am walking, I am sitting, I am chanting." And there is also a deeper self which most people are not aware of—the self that knows this. When you are walking, when you are going to the supermarket or going to the movies, you think, "I am going, I am going, I am going." You don't realize that every step that your body takes has something that is knowing that your body is taking that step. For every breath that you take, the breathing activity does not know that it is breathing. There is a knower of the breathing activity.

This body that is walking and breathing is walking a path. This body that walks and breathes and talks is walking on a trail, and the name of that trail is "Birth, growth, old age, decay, and death." That is the trail that every one of us is walking. One may think, "Now I'm going to college, now I'm going to a career, now I'm going to be a famous writer, a famous musician." This is all part of the path. You are walking down the path, and you come to college thinking, "Oh, this is the time to be stressed out, this is the time to meet people." Then you go into a career: "Oh, this is the time where I am supposed to be fulfilled." Then you come to a place called retirement, the golden years, so that when you are seventy-five years old, you can hit a little round ball on the grass.

This is the path that life is. It is not that you achieve anything—nothing is permanent, you are always moving, and all the time something deeper than that is within you. True self, or the God, or the Kingdom of Heaven is within you. And what the Kingdom of Heaven does, what the God does, is to be aware of you. God is the pure knowing.

If you take up a meditation practice, what you are trying to become aware of is that your mind is identifying itself as the body, and says, "This is what I am; I am David, I am Sue." The mind, which is identifying itself as the body, is going to be informed that it actually exists in another mode as well, which is the awareness of the body. The practice is essential and very simple. The reason it is simple is that it does not require the thinking activity.

When you come into the meditation hall—and as your practice deepens, this includes anything that happens in life, not just in the meditation hall—things are precise and simple, very straightforward. You don't have a choice of how you take your tea or how your body is postured. Even if you have your cell phone in your pocket, you cannot text. This is called the nontexting posture. It was not always called the nontexting posture, but nowadays it might be called the nontexting posture. The mind cannot control the body, saying, "Let's go here, let's go there, I want to do this, I want to do that, what do I do now?" The mantra of the thinking activity is, "What's next?" That is its mode of operation; it cannot rest in the present moment. When it rests, it dissolves, and in that dissolution, in that moment, the mind awakens to its original luminosity, which had been obscured by thinking.

The practice is, when you walk, be aware of walking. When you are sitting here, use your will to make contact with the body, instead of to converse about it. There is a term in our tradition called the sword of wisdom. You learn to exercise the sword of wisdom, so that wisdom changes the object you are experiencing from the mental gossip to the physical body—that is the wisdom practice. When you are walking and you are daydreaming about this and that, wisdom says, no, come back to walking. That walking is now your mode of existence, you are existing currently in the present moment. You are aware of walking, and the awareness that you did not know existed before starts to come within range of your own experience.

I am now old. I am at the end of the walk. And once upon a time, I had a good basketball jump shot. When I was younger—was that "me," or is "me" the old guy? And if you say it is the same guy, what is the same, what part is the same? Not a single cell, not a single nerve, not a single synapse. There is no connection, but there is a chain of causation. If you take an apple seed, plant it in the ground, water it, and watch it become a tree, is the seed the same as the tree? No. Is it different from the tree? One can't even answer a question like that, it doesn't make sense. There are no words to describe the conditions of being of anything.

There is something constant through all these years, and that is the light that is illuminating you. Once you enter the spiritual path, your life is no longer about fulfilling your individuality; that is an impossible thing. Your individuality is a journey from a womb to a coffin. Regardless of how much money you have, regardless of how much fame you have, regardless of how accomplished you are as an athlete or a musician, this is the path. Spiritual wisdom says that if you make that individuality into something very important, you will have difficulty with its inevitable disintegration. You will fear it, because you have thought, "What I am is now disappearing."

There is within you that which is beyond birth and death, beyond success and failure. It just knows that you are, and it is. When you come into the zendo and make a bow, know that this is not the place where individuality is important, this is a place where individuality is humbled. "Whenever I associate with others may I view myself as the lowest of all." Very different from teachings at the university and the college, or teachings in the office where you are under the pressure of being rated, and your worth is based on performance. No, as a performer you are impermanent, don't make a fuss. Before you have to exit stage left, you should realize that within you is that which is eternal, which is unaffected, which is present within all things as the core of their being, and which is pure spirit, completely nonmaterial.

How do you become aware of the inner illumination? How do you become aware that there is a deeper knower? The path will always be in the present moment. It will always be when "I" stops, when the mind stops. Society devalues moments of stopping. But these are actually the great moments. When the thinking mind is not present, the song of a bird is wonderful, and something smiles on you—the basic simplicity. You experience the all-pervading goodness of your own being when it is not being tormented by the obsession with personal affairs.

For those of you who are beginning the practice, when breathing in, be aware of breathing in; putting on your coat, be aware of putting on your coat; putting on your shoes, be aware. And smile at how pleasant it is when your existence is that simple. You have not been put here to be judged or to prove your self-worth. Your self-worth is that you exist. You have already fulfilled your purpose for being here by hearing a bird or seeing a snowflake. That miraculous activity is your fulfillment—please do not miss it.

19

In Humility, Not in Things

WHAT YOU ARE DOING in meditation practice is quite simple. It is training the mind to think in accordance with reality, instead of in accordance with a mistaken notion of reality. I heard this week that a famous Zen teacher passed away. When a teacher passes away, or someone you love passes away, that is a very important message to us. We may be creating a life based on not passing away. By not acknowledging our passing away, we are taking ourselves seriously, as a vessel that can find permanent happiness.

If that is the way we are thinking about life, we are not thinking in accordance with how things actually are. Because of that, we may have to go through two experiences that we may not want to go through. One is sorrow, the other is fear. Those two experiences are the inevitable result of a mind that thinks in accordance with reality being other than the way it is. Spiritual life should teach us that happiness is found in humility, and not in things, that happiness is found in serving the happiness of others, happiness is found in, "Love thy neighbor as thyself." These are the true teachings based on the idea that we should not try to find meaningful happiness as an independent self.

As an independent self, we are going to go through the experience of the dissolution of what we take ourselves to be. If our whole life is about ourselves, then when the self is no longer coherent, we will think that it is a problem, that it is tragic. We take such pride in how well we do things, how beautiful we look, how smart we are, how together we get things—this is called taking pride in things that we are going to lose. In other words, we are taking refuge in sorrow and fear. The dharma teachings are quite happy. In the beginning, they sound depressing, but when you actually live in accordance with them, you will realize that the way you have been living your life is so neurotic, it is comic.

The arrogance of the self-based life is an astonishing thing. The mind has been conditioned by generations of ignorance. It takes courage to go against the ideas that you have been fed almost since birth—that this whole universe is about your performance in it; you are here to be judged, you are here to prove yourself. Some of you recently had a parent die or had a brother on the verge of not being able to escape an illness, or you've read the news. What did you learn from that experience? Did you learn anything from that? Did it tell you that this is something that you are going to experience? Did it let you start reflecting a little bit?

What is the point of this stress we impose upon ourselves, when we are simply going to walk the same path that our mothers and our fathers walked? We are going to have to go through that experience, and that experience is our fundamental teacher, not our enemy. It is a reminder of our own impermanence. When you start to untangle this web of self-importance, you discover the natural grace of being. Slowly, over time, you gain the insight that the thinking activity, the personal self, is not your home. The thinking activity is just an activity running around inside you. And there is a deeper self that has been born into the thinking activity.

This is the whole of the spiritual insight—to discover that you can relax when you hear the wind blow. You can let go when you hear the crows squawking, you can let go of the thinking activity and discover peace. Discover a light heart, discover how simple your existence was meant to be. It was never about what you have been told it is. It is about a visit to this world, because that is what existence is. Existence is the appearance and disappearance of individual forms. Your thinking mind should shift—it should become soft, it should become kind, it should become humble, it should become grateful. It should allow you to enter the present moment, illuminated by the original source of light.

Perhaps I think about these things more these days because the impermanence deity travels with me. When you carry the impermanence deity with you, you also become acquainted with the permanent deity. Many people are worshipping the impermanent deity, whose name is ultimately sorrow and fear. And there is the permanent deity that is illuminating our mind activity—true self, the Buddha mind, God, or the source of existence. It is beholding you and is always with you. We turn our backs to it because we have this education about life that everything is measured by me. Everything you do in life is witnessed by your own divinity, but instead, the thinking activity steals it for its own advantage.

20

Nancy and Charlie

THE WHOLE OF THE SPIRITUAL PATH, the source of all religious wisdom, arises from seeing just how it is that you are sitting on the cushion. But it has to be looked at with a sensitive and humble mind. If your mind is absorbed in self-concerns, then what you experience sitting on the cushion is self-concern. My existence becomes, "I think, therefore I am." And because I am thinking, I am existing. This is what is called ignorance, because the situation is not being seen accurately. If your mind will leave you alone for a minute, you will see that the thinking activity has no one in it. It is just a movie that is playing for the consciousness. And it gives rise to this idea that there is an actual entity living inside your body—not because there is, but because your thinking is asserting that there is.

This is deeply seated within each one of us, because when we were born, perhaps our parents had been looking through name books for months. "If it's a boy we'll call him Charlie, and if it's a girl we'll call her Nancy." And you were in there listening, so the trouble started right away! You weren't Charlie or Nancy, you were mommy; you had no separate existence. You were just one of her things—her elbow, her arm, her fetus. You did not exist; you were not a separate entity. Then you appeared in the world and the umbilical cord was cut. You were informed that you are Charlie or Nancy, that you are existing separate from your mother, and you are separate from every other creature. You were told you were now a self.

After that you went to kindergarten to prove you could get the most stars, and you went to high school, trying to be the teacher's pet. And if you couldn't be the teacher's pet, you became a bad boy or bad girl, so at least you'd get some kind of attention. Then all kinds of trouble follow—until you end up old like me, which is the culmination of all your problems!

This is the human situation. This is why people who see the human predicament shed tears, because people are struggling. You see fellow human beings struggling, trying to find fulfillment as an individual when that is absolutely impossible. Human life is like Sisyphus, forever rolling a rock up a hill and having it roll back down, and that's if you're lucky. All that happens because the mind intervened between the consciousness and the body and claimed to be the self. It misinterpreted what is taking place. That is why we do these odd things—sitting still, walking in a line, and keeping quiet. We do these activities just to allow a glimpse of how reality looks when the mind is not intervening between the consciousness and the body.

What you actually see when the mind is quieted and you are experiencing how reality looks at that moment, what you see at that point, is the body. When the mind is standing between consciousness and the body, what you experience is the mind, you don't experience the body. So, if the mind is blue, you say, "Everything is blue." If the mind is depressed, you say, "Oh, life is depressing." The mind is what you are seeing. But with quiet mind, the experience becomes, "Breathing in, I am aware of

breathing in. Breathing out, I am aware of breathing out."
What does it mean to be aware of breathing in, breathing out? It means to be aware of the body, because your entire body is an extension of that experience. Feel the breathing, feel your arms and your legs, feel your belly rising and falling.

What does all that mean? It means that the mind is saying, "I exist as the body," but the consciousness is now seeing the body as an object that it experiences. I'll say that again. The mind is pointing to the body as its self. The thinking activity is identifying its essence as the physical form, "This is what I am." When we go around in a casual way in the human world saying, "Who am I? I am this," we don't realize that is an activity of the thinking mind.

When your practice matures and you get disenchanted with the thinking mind, or the thinking mind runs out of energy, the deeper view emerges. And the mind, which has become clear to allow the penetration of the consciousness into the body, is now rising with new data. The last time the mind got information about what it was, it was Nancy. That was the last program it received: "I am Nancy, therefore I should figure out my life based on my being Nancy." Consequently, all the thinking the mind did was constructed on this "I am Nancy" platform. Now the mind, for the first time, gets new information—that is why it is called a spiritual rebirth, that is why it is called being reborn in the spirit. The mind gets reborn, it gets a new program. This body that it has been identifying as itself is an object that it experiences. It is the beholder of the body, the knower of the body.

The mind that said, "I am Nancy" is now different. Now it's a case of, "I became a human being from the falling into the thinking activity. I was born from the transcendent knower." Transcendent does not mean far away, for the purposes of our talk transcendent just means you cannot find it anywhere. There is no place to find the essence of consciousness because it is the only thing that knows. It cannot be known; we have no place from which to look at it—it is looking at us. People cannot see the original consciousness, because as an existing creature we are what it falls into. My teacher used to say, "A human being cannot see the Golden Buddha, and the Golden Buddha cannot see a human being." That is why it says in the scriptures that the source of your existence cannot be known, but it can be realized. The Buddha explained that it is realized by people who treat others as themselves.

The mind had been creating your life based on the idea that what you are is inside the skin, and everything else in the universe is outside of the skin. But now, you are not inside your skin anymore, you are the beholder. This doesn't negate that we exist—we do exist in this world as individuals. But how did we get here, how did we become this individual? Track down how you came into existence. If you examined a sperm, you would not find yourself in it, and you would not find yourself in an egg. These are just physical secretions that when they interact grow into a human being, the same way the stamen and pistil of the flower of an apple tree create a fertilized seed and that seed grows into an apple tree, the fertilized seed grows into a human being. But where do "I" exist inside that human being?

See that you have been born in this world, but not into the body; you have been born into the thinking activity—that is how you were birthed. You were birthed by the thinking activity being informed that it was the body, when in truth the thinking activity has no self in it. Your original nature is divine, your original nature is illuminating consciousness prior to thinking. I try not to make it sound fancy, because it isn't physics, it isn't science; it is a revelation. It is very logical in its own way, but it does not require thinking. All you have to do is be aware or bring the mind back home.

The mind has been wandering around in this world of I am Nancy, I am Charlie, and it is wandering, wandering, wandering, trying to find meaning, while all the time searching outside itself. That is what it does, it is just wandering around trying to get organized, but it can never get itself organized because it is always driven by this and that. It is like the prodigal child in the Bible. Bring your mind back home, so that with full awareness, the mind is not running away from being with you. One moment, mind and body together, one moment, engaged in walking meditation and realizing that you are aware of walking while you are walking. One moment, and your body becomes empty of self and illuminated by consciousness. The structure of your existence is shifted, and you become attuned to the deeper knower within you. This is the feast to which the prodigal son returns. And you smile.

Before saying a few last words, I just want to ask if this is not clear to anyone. Is it possible that this is not clear? If it is not clear, please ask. And if it is clear, you will live in peace as you go through life and death. Because death is the dissolution of the thinking activity, which was not the identity after all. Nancy dies, Charlie dies, because Nancy and Charlie were words, words have no being. Most people are not stable, because they are just words. It doesn't really help you at all to understand this, it just eases the burden. You cannot win, you cannot prove yourself. While your appearance in this universe is temporary, it is the most blessed miraculous thing that could ever happen. You are now experiencing the most blessed grace that any being can possibly experience, and you have forgotten.

Transcendent consciousness is the only true existence. Now it has been born as you—you are existing by the grace of that birth. You have eyes, ears, nose, tongue, body, and mind. And because you are a human being, your mind can experience the wisdom insight that the source of all existence is one being—you can realize that. You cannot experience it—you can realize it but not have it as an object of experience. You can melt back into it. This dissolving into the oneness of being is essentially Zen practice, but *you* cannot do it because you cannot dissolve yourself.

When you love so completely, when you give yourself completely to what you are experiencing, the mind disappears from its position between you and what you are experiencing. That is why there is a love and a beauty and an elegance to the whole of spiritual life. You have to do something so lovely, so self-effacing, so magical. You have to make the barking of a dog more important than your mental conversation. You have to make the song of a bird more important than your term paper.

Mind Is the Holy Land

THIS YEAR, 2018, IS A NOTEWORTHY CALENDAR YEAR for me, because it duplicates the calendar of 1991. In that year, March 31 was Passover, and April 1 was Easter—they came right in a row. And it was a blue moon, because when the full moon occurs on the 30th or the 31st, it's a blue moon, the second full moon of the month. And that was the night that our house burned down—on the night of the full moon, the blue moon. Over Passover, Easter, twenty-seven years ago, our house burned down. That is always a poignant memory. When we lose something, it is also a reminder of how little we actually need.

The season of Passover and Easter is a time when religions engage in rituals. In religion there is no real sense of the esoteric meaning of the ritual, it is just ritual. You do it because it's been done for thousands of years. The idea of whether it actually makes sense is rarely considered. If you look at things from a deeper view, the idea of going out of the land of slavery on Passover is similar to awakening from the body being the totality of the identity—it is the same idea. And the idea of dying and then being resurrected—dying is the dissolution of the self, and resurrection is the unborn mind awakening. But you don't resurrect as a body. Because people only know themselves as bodies, they think they must resurrect as a body. But people don't realize that even just by sitting on the cushion you may experience death and resurrection, you may experience going out of the land of Egypt. These are actual insights that you can have about the structure of your own existence. Personally, I've never been too fond of rituals, except, perhaps, the ones that include chocolate. Holidays where you get chocolate are good, but if you are only getting a hard-boiled egg or a piece of Matzoh? There should be a holiday where you fulfill God's will by having baklava!

One of the things you are learning in the practice of meditation is that to be at peace with your psychological condition is to your extreme benefit. When you experience your mental states, if you experience torment or anger it means it is time to relax. And if you can be with these states in a relaxed, nonrejecting mood, their energies will melt and flow. You are sitting with your own mind, and the mind is creating a tormented response to life. It is no different from sticking your hand in the fire and saying, "What should I do—it hurts! What should I do—I need to look in a holy book. What should I do—my hand is burning! What should I do—my mind is burning!"

What should you do? Become a more intelligent human being and create mental states that are pleasant to experience, or at least stop reacting to the unpleasant ones. Some people listen to unintelligent logic. Unintelligent logic is logic that justifies negative emotions. Nobody is ever angry without a reason, so now you have given yourself a reason. "I should hold my hand in the fire because it's good for me, I should hold anger in my mind because look what they did to me." How many people think that way? "I should hold anger; I should not forgive." These are not particularly religious teachings, unless you call common sense religion.

Your mind will be your companion until the day you die—your most intimate companion—closer than your lover, closer than your iPhone, closer than anything is your mind. You could be sitting on the cushion here, you could be sitting on the cushion in Hawaii, you could be sitting on the cushion anywhere. But the content of your mind is going to be with you wherever you go. Yet people rarely think, "I am creating the quality of my life by whether my mind is at peace with my life. It is creating suffering because it has never been trained." Or "I never received the teaching that how I think is the quality of my life." Please consider that.

The esoteric teachings of Passover or Easter are teachings that say that the true nature of the mind is beyond thinking. The essence of your existence is not contained within the thinking activity and is not contained within the body; it is beyond thinking and abides as the essence of you. This essence of you is with you or is you forever. Beyond where you live or when you live, any being who ever existed arises from the same essence.

I am in a situation where this body's continued existence is fragile. If I hadn't met my teachers, there would be no escape. But there is an escape. When ego or thinking dissolves, the deeper self reveals itself. It shines and says, "Here I am within you and you overlooked me, you overlooked your own self." Your life was taking place in the land of Egypt, you were a human being where you were subject to birth, growth, old age, decay, and death—that was your slavery. But illuminating it for the entire time was the deeper essence.

I would encourage you to live an intelligent life. Nowadays people are in grave danger because instead of making friends with the mind, people are taught to anesthetize the mind, they are afraid to be alone with themselves without technology. Buddhism is not a religion or a belief system. Buddhism is deep common sense. There is with us this activity called the thinking activity. The same way that we have eyes, ears, a nose, a tongue, a body, we have a thinking activity. Base the thinking activity on forgiveness and kindness and sincerity, because the state of the mind is sacred. That is the true holy land; your mind is the holy land.

If we think a country is the holy land, we get into fights over the holy land because we think it is a thing, and then our holy land becomes a violent place. The holy land is our own mind—we are always walking around with the holy land, we are always walking around with the most sacred, but we are defiling it. We are allowing our holy land to become defiled with aggression, we are allowing our holy land to become defiled with anger, we are allowing our holy land to become defiled by depression. We are allowing those principles to operate in the holy land instead of principles such as, *Whenever I associate with others, may I view myself as the lowest of all. Even if someone I have helped harms me without any reason, may I see them as my holy spiritual guide. If someone out of jealousy harms me or insults me, may I take defeat upon myself and offer them the victory.* All of those teachings from the Buddhist texts are designed to purify the holy land.

22

Here I Am

THE PURPOSE OF ZAZEN practice is not to have some tidbit of spirituality included in our life. The purpose is that our whole life should become workable. We go through this process in the meditation hall of being relaxed and accepting of the mind's chatter, allowing it to calm down enough to know that we are sitting here and breathing. "Here I am." And this "here I am" experience never *isn't* there. We can see that whenever we release the thinking activity and come into an intimate experience of the body, we experience: "Here I am, now I am present." If we really grasp what is going on, we start to have some confidence that every situation in life never affects that fundamental structure. If we let go of thinking and experience the body, we experience an authentic presence: *Here I am.* It is authentic because it is not dependent on whether things are going well or poorly. The intimacy of the consciousness, the experiencer, and the body will always bring a moment of authentic being.

Most people have no idea that there is this eternal inner radiance or goodness. I say eternal, not in the sense that it lasts for a long time; it is eternal because in every moment of time, that's how it is. It is this goodness that is the only true fulfillment. The thinking activity is always based on fulfillment being what's next. "If I could get a job with a nonprofit, I would be happy forever. If I could find a way to pay my school loans, I would be free of misery. If only I didn't have this pain, if only I didn't have this or that. Then, once I complete that, I'll finally be at peace." And that moment never comes. It's always what's next. This is how the thinking activity functions—that fulfillment is always in the future.

I remember when my teacher came with me to a maximum-security prison where we had a sitting group, and he gave a talk to the inmates. It was during the time that Ronald Reagan was president, and he said to them, "You know, when you breathe in you will know more pleasure than Ronald Reagan knows being president." He was telling this to inmates. Astonishing! He was telling them how you bring some light into hell, just like that.

This is how you should cultivate yourself to make your life more spiritualized. It means that you are no longer coming into life as a beggar, you are no longer coming into life thinking that a relationship, a job, money, or whatever is going to do it for you. You come in already done, you come in as, "Here I am." And this "I" is not the ego or personal self. It is an impersonal presence. You will notice over time that there is nothing you can do to produce that experience, you can only allow it because it is your own nature. What do you have to do to see the sun rise in the morning? What do you have to do to hear a bird? What do you have to do to experience peace of mind? They are beyond our capacity to produce through our own will and our own effort because they are innate.

Everything we do as an individual disappears. We are a temporary appearance. So, give up the idea of complaining about what is happening because a complaining mind is of little benefit. It is not a healthy way to go through life. You start to see that pride is comical and humility is filled with grace. It is obvious. When you live your life in that way, you will find yourself reinforced by this universe's kindness. This universe provides oxygen and water. This universe gives us toes, an immune system, and ears. This universe gives us life—it loves us, and all it is asking is *cut it out* and stop aggressively trying to prove our worth. It is taking care of us. In fact, we are all one.

If you see a child suffering because of its own mistakes, you want to say, "Why are you doing this to yourself? Your life is a gift, it is a miracle. Why are you creating these goals that leave you feeling you are not worthy of love, not worthy of happiness, if you don't fulfill them? Why are you doing this to yourself?" The whole universe is saying that to you. Birds are saying that to you, trees are saying that to you, and chocolate chip muffins are saying that to you also. Please think about this being what your practice is, this being what your spiritual life is. You don't need Buddhism, you don't need Zen, you don't need Christianity, Judaism, Islam—you don't need any of that. You just need to be simple, kind, grateful, and have the light that is within you penetrate through your egoism. That is enough.

23

Don't Let Yourself Off the Hook

WAS TALKING THIS WEEK with a friend from a different religious tradition. He told me that the end of times is near and that if I could just accept certain beliefs, after death I would be able to resurrect in the peak of youth, never be ill again, and live for all eternity. I was thinking, "Why did I get stuck with Zen? This sounds like a much better deal!"

One of the things you should do in zazen practice is to not let yourself off the hook like that. You should find your own salvation by becoming bored with your own suffering. You should not try to fix your mind doing zazen, except perhaps the activity called "like and dislike." There should be nothing arising within you that you reject. There should be nothing inside you that makes you uncomfortable.

That does not mean that there are not difficult things, or that you might become undermined. But if you abandon like and dislike and just allow your mind to arise with all its hopes and wishes and laments, and make friends with it, it will eventually calm. This does not produce a normal kind of paradise. It does not produce some beautiful state of mind. You feel you can be a genuine human being; you don't have to pretend things are other than the way they are. You don't have to fake it; you don't have to put chocolate icing on it. You are just there, solid, accepting yourself as you are. You no longer need to pretend.

In this state, you discover what has been with you all along—an illumination that you cannot describe. You can call it "no self" or "pure consciousness." You just know that when you stop rejecting or trying to fix your human condition, you become authentic. There is no problem; there is nothing in your life that has ruined your life except the activity of like and dislike. Even if you experience profound self-loathing for horrible mistakes you may have made, or if you experience anger for things that happened to you, those things are not in and of themselves problematic. The only problem is that we constantly try to distract ourselves from experiencing them. We take up imaginary heavens, like iTunes: "As long as I can listen to something, I won't have to look at my mental content." Instead of becoming authentic, we become addicted to something that is going to take our minds off our inability to make friends with the part of ourselves that we reject. We are too distracted; we cannot meet the mind and bow to it.

The truth is that these states are arising within us, but they don't threaten us unless we like and dislike them, or get swept away with them. This is why zazen practice is such a wonderful, horrible situation. You sit here, and you are giving up all your props to spend a couple hours defenseless against your psychological content. You should accept yourself; you should know your content very intimately. You should know it without any desire for it to go away—all the things that you think bother you or that you wish were some other way. You should become intimate with them so that they arise, and arise, and arise, and stop producing any reaction. It is always the reaction, the suppression, the like and dislike that produce stress.

We are about to go into a sesshin. The sesshin is about taking time to learn how to surf your mind, learning how to allow the parts of your mind that have been suppressed so that you could pass your interviews to get your job—because if you told them what you were really like, you would not stand a chance—allowing them to arise and dissolve. The part of you that you cannot let anybody know about comes to visit you. And all you can do is to accept it. It is all right to be defenseless. It is all right to be completely comfortable with yourself. This is the spiritual path. Be comfortable with your mind—whether healthy or sick, living or dying, in love or brokenhearted. If you can be alone with yourself, you can be comfortable anywhere.

24

The Mirror of Your Body

THE PURPOSE OF SPIRITUAL PRACTICE is to undo the damage that the thinking activity inflicts upon itself. Many of the difficulties that people experience in life come from the thinking activity reacting in unskilled ways to the circumstances of life. When the mind comes into the meditation hall, it is unaccustomed to being irrelevant to the basic simplicity of the present moment. The thinking activity cannot be that which is aware of the breathing. And it is unaccustomed to being aware of its true nature because it has been immersed for so long in the thinking activity.

What is this fundamental activity that thinking performs that creates problems in human life? It asserts that it exists separate from the universe. That activity creates a false self, a psychological self that has no actual basis. The thinking activity is the source of all individualized being. Everything that has a name adheres to and arises in the mind; it is the mind appearing, and the thinking activity conceives that the trillions upon trillions of things that exist are all separate entities. Based on that error, it tries to create a satisfactory existence for itself by organizing those trillions and trillions of things to be the way it would like them to be. Big task.

This whole universe is one vast, undivided organism, yet the human race is destroying this world. Why? Because the human mind is based on everything having a separate existence: "This universe is separate from me. The people are separate from me. If I love somebody, even that person is separate from me." That's why there is so little softness in this world, so little love.

If you want to experience holiness, then regard all things, including yourself, as one interpenetrating body. The thinking activity says, "I am existing only within this body, and everything outside this body is separate from me. Therefore, who cares what happens, it has nothing fundamentally to do with me."

The deep spiritual wisdom which you approach through calming the mind and seeing its original nature will someday manifest to you—the wisdom of the true seat of existence, the true self. Different from the thinking activity, the true self appears when beholding breathing in and beholding breathing out. When that instant arises, you realize your body is illuminated by that which knows it. When we are doing zazen, we are undoing the illusory "damage" to the consciousness that has fallen into the thinking activity and forgotten its transcendent nature.

I hope you can cultivate the wisdom experience in your practice. And if you can't cultivate it in your practice, then cultivate lovingkindness and the ability not to respond with aggression when life is other than the way you would want it to be. Cultivate the knowing that everything you experience has yourself within. The thinking activity says that things are separate from you, but the wisdom says this is all one interpenetrating activity taking place in the mirror of your bodymind. Your bodymind is a mirror in which the universe exists.

Treat things in a beautiful way, and your mind will become beautiful. Treat things in an egotistical way, and you will have difficulty coping with circumstances that are not the way you want them to be. Do you understand this teaching somewhat? I hope so.

When you look into someone's eyes, you should understand that ultimately there is nobody inside that thing you are looking at—there is no one in there. It seems like you are looking at somebody—you think they are in there behind their eyes and I am in here behind these eyes, and we are having a transcendent meeting. But really, you look into someone's eyes, and you are still outside of them. In this universe, we are walking in the light of heaven. Our whole life is living in the light of heaven and dying in the light of heaven. You can't catch this experience in words. But I hope maybe when you go walking sometime, you will realize you are aware of walking. Everywhere is the same: beautiful, peaceful, illuminated.

25

The Blessed States

THE WISDOM TEACHING of our tradition is astonishing to the ordinary human mind—that's why it is difficult to understand. There are parts of the teaching that are easy to comprehend because they are obvious, such as when you treat people with kindness, you will have a more pleasant state of mind than when you treat people with aggression. That teaching is actually the basis of the ethics of a nontheistic tradition. As Christ said, "Turn the other cheek." This is not based on the commandment of God; it is based on basic intelligence, on common sense. If you base ethics on natural intelligence, you realize that how your mind functions is what determines the quality of your life.

If we cultivate what are called the blessed states—compassion, sympathy, tranquility, and lovingkindness—we will experience their blessedness. These states are self-authenticating. We don't need someone to say, "You must do this because it is the will of God." And it is also very clear that if you stress your mind out, you will be in a state of stress. And that if you get angry, you will experience being angry.

If we want to have an intelligence functioning, we must be aware of what is going on in our minds, not only in our circumstances. What is going to determine the quality of our life isn't how fast we drive to the next place. What is going to determine the quality of our life is the mood with which we are driving. And it's the same with walking—if the mind is busy in the future, we lose track of its mood in the present moment.

If we want to cultivate ourselves spiritually, our foot-steps should be peaceful, our hearts open and grateful that we are actually cultivating the blessedness within us. This part of the teaching may be difficult to practice, but at least it's comprehensible.

The wisdom teachings say that composite things—things that are composed of parts—don't have a soul, a fixed center point, an "I." This is the deep teaching, designed to free one from the most fundamental error the mind is making, and to expose it to its true original nature—its ultimate nonexistence. So, let's examine this teaching.

Start with a simple structure like a meditation hall. This meditation hall appears to exist, but it has no soul. In the absolute sense, there is no entity called "meditation hall"—it is a name given to a particular shape and func-tion. When you put in sheetrock and an altar, wiring and windows, and people come to meditate in that place, we call it a meditation hall. But it is composed of parts and produced by causes. It doesn't have its own will; it doesn't have its own beingness. The meditation hall exists as a concept in the mind that is naming it. The mind has a concept in it, "meditation hall," and that concept is what exists. The meditation hall doesn't self-exist—it is mani-fested by the thinking activity.

The same holds true when we see a cloud. The cloud is there, but it doesn't have a soul; it doesn't self-exist. It is a temporary appearance, something produced by water, heat, air, and sunshine. We say "a cloud," but if we want to know where a cloud exists, it exists in the thinking activity that puts a name on it. Extending this a little further, if we try to understand the existence of a tree—branches, trunk, roots, and leaves—these all are activities of the tree. The tree is an activity, a circulation of fire, earth, air, and water. Where would the "self," the unmoving essence of the tree be situated? There is no self in there that we can actually find, even though we can nevertheless commune with the incredible complexity of the structure.

One of the composite things that exists through being named is a human being, the most complex of structures. And that naming creates it as an entity instead of an activity, and places a soul, an "I am," inside it. As human beings, we appear will-lessly, by causation. The union of a sperm and an egg evolves in a will-less chain of causation that follows a path called birth, growth, old age, decay, and death. As human beings, we are more complex than a meditation hall or a cloud or a tree. We have layers of functions such as sense organs, will, abstract thinking, etc. But each of these is produced by causes, each is without a soul, an unchanging self.

Everything is produced by causes. Everything is the flowing of the energy of this universe. This universe gives rise out of itself to these temporary forms. One of the activities it is giving rise to is a human being, and one of the will-less functions that resides in a human being is the thinking activity. But instead of it realizing, "I am one with the universe, I am manifested together with every-thing," the thinking activity says, "I am separate from the universe." This is the human condition. We are originally one with the universe, but the thinking mind has been named, and it identifies itself by this name, the same way a cloud is named, or a meditation hall is named, or a tree is named—by the mind naming it. This mind has received its name from parents that inform it, "You exist as a separate entity. You are not a temporary flowing appearance of the universe." It is as if a wave was told it is separate from the ocean. One can say the whole of the spiritual path is to restore the damage that has come over the mind as a result of this mistaken idea.

The mind has been functioning under the delusion that it can fulfill itself separately from everything that gave rise to it. It is given existence by food and water and sunshine and oxygen and everything else that goes into the incredible structure of a human being. It is an expression of the universe giving rise to forms because that is what the universe does. The force that moves the universe is cause and effect, or karma, and the mind has lost track of that. The name of that error, specifically, is, "I am." The thinking activity says, "I am existing inside this body," instead of, "I am existing as one with everything. That is my original nature."

If we can have some sense that we and everything that exists are one interpenetrating organism which has performed the astonishing activity of producing sense organs that enable the universe to see its self, we will see that the whole of existence is the miraculous activity of the self seeing itself. That insight will allow the meaning of our birth to become clear. Our mission here on planet Earth is to know that we are children of the universe and, as individuals, are temporary. We are temporary forms in which the universe is both expressing and experiencing itself. The totality of existence has given rise to us in order to experience itself. That is completely beyond any personal meaning—but, sorry, that is the truth.

Life is not about whether you become a millionaire. The universe does not exist for any reason other than to celebrate its own existence by allowing you to be. That should be the heart of a Zen student: *I woke up this morning, thank you.* Who are we saying thank you to? Well, we can say thank you to God, that is okay: Thank you, God. We can also say thank you to the whole universe, which birthed our existence. We can say thank you to our pancreas, or our lungs, or our heart. But say thank you to something, because we did not get here on our own, and we are going to disappear before too long.

Stay humble, stay soft, stay playful, live in the blessed states instead of the stressed-out states. The stressed-out, angry, difficult states of mind are founded on this thinking: *I am separate from the universe, and I am searching for that which will fulfill me.* That mistake in the mind is the root of every problem.

Someone once asked the Buddha, "Do we suffer because of our own actions, or because of the actions of others, or does suffering happen randomly?" The Buddha said, "No, we suffer because we identify ourselves incorrectly."

What Is Zen?

THERE IS A GREAT DIFFERENCE between a word and what that word signifies. For example, the distance is vast between the term "full moon" and the actual full moon, or the word "kiss" and an actual kiss. The distance between the term "Zen" and the experience the word is meant to express is even more vast, as it is intended to convey an insight that is so splendid, so profound, yet so paradoxically ordinary that the human mind cannot approach it. It points to a reality that overturns or shatters the most fundamental of all assumptions: that there is an authentic reality, a self, within each human form.

The historical Buddha, when he first awakened to the deeper truth, thought to remain silent because what he had realized was too subtle for others to grasp. Later, he reconsidered and uttered the courageous, noble truth: that the human condition is an incomplete state, a fallen state, that can be transcended. This is what we inadequately express with the term "Zen," though in truth, we should make nine bows before uttering the word.

The mind (or, one might say, an individual) becomes interested in Zen when it meets an event that it has difficulty integrating. In simple terms, when a relationship breaks up, when a serious illness or accident occurs, and it appears as though the path to personal happiness and fulfillment is cut off, the ordinary human mind has difficulty coping and seeks comfort from a new source. This may lead to some form of therapy or a neurotic distraction—or, out of some desperation, an interest in meditation. Even the historical Buddha became interested in Zen only when he saw a human corpse for the first time in his life. Because of his extraordinary sensitivity, he realized in his bones that he would eventually have to go through that experience himself. He realized that the experience of death could not be addressed by a princely life of pleasure and privilege.

Ordinarily, people are driven by the pursuit of happiness—whether it takes the form of a lover, a career, fame, approval of parents or peers—and that implies that happiness, an "inner" experience, is produced by external circumstances. In order to make sense of this pursuit, the mind has to hide the evidence that this is an enormous error—it has to hide the inevitability of its own impermanence, its inescapable death. This is the "normal" human condition, where death is regarded as taboo, as too depressing to think about, when in truth, fundamental sanity is impossible when the mind is not in accord with the impermanent nature of all things. Hence, in cultures like these, there are high levels of stress and neurosis from ignoring reality. People take refuge in drugs and alcohol or hide from the world by focusing on their cell phones to suppress or distract from the anxiety levels caused by the futile pursuit of happiness.

Very few take up the path of looking deeply into the structure of human being to be able to integrate impermanence. Very few. We can use "Zen" to refer to this path of radical inquiry into the nature of being. When

Shakyamuni Buddha was first stunned by the experience of impermanence, he left home, inspired by this thought: "What if I were to search for that which underlies all becoming, for the unsurpassed perfect security which is nirvana, the perfect freedom of the unconditioned state?"

The path that the Buddha walked was to examine every element of personal existence to see precisely what the self was or what and where "I" dwelt. The mind was used to examine the subjective side of reality—the body, the senses, and the mind—to see where "I" is situated in that structure. After years of this practice, the Buddha's consciousness—that which was examining the subjectivity—penetrated through every aspect and could not discover an "I" within it.

He realized, in meditative insight, that since the body and mind could be objectified, they could not be the self. Even the sense organs, such as the eyes, do not ultimately contain within them a self-essence that is performing the act of seeing. An existing self is created through thinking which, in essence, is without a self or a substance.

This insight is described in the opening of the Heart Sutra: "The Blessed One saw that all the components of ego, of individualized existence, were empty of a true self and was thus saved from all suffering and distress." The experience may also be described as the mind awakening from a reality in which all sentient beings are self-existing and separate, to a reality in which all sentient beings are produced by karma and conditions (i.e., without will but by an endless chain of causation that extends throughout the entire universe)—and that the existence of an actual, separate self is a mistaken, temporary view of reality. In truth, all of existence is an interpenetrating oneness manifested and illuminated by One Mind. This was expressed over and over by the Buddha. The cause of suffering is the mind's attachment or identification of true, transcendent being as a form that is impermanent. "In all its parts, both small and infinite, this one transcended his own life's history. Composed and calm, he broke apart, like a shell of armor, all that makes the self."

This does not mean that there is no true self, but rather that it is not contained within the dualistic realm of subject and object. The true nature is unborn, or unmanifested, yet it is that which "knows" everything.

The spiritual path then becomes the maturing of the mind from the false, subjective assumption of self to the awakened state where the mind realizes the ultimate "emptiness" of all things. This takes the form of consistently humbling and negating the aggressive tendencies that arise from the limited view of self which interprets the universe as an object separate from itself. In the great view, the psychological activity that has created the individual self dissolves, and along with it, the subject/object dichotomy. This allows the realization of the majestic, noble view that the entire universe is one interpenetrating body with no separate self-existence. The mind that is borne forth from this wisdom is the one that proclaims, "Love thy neighbor as thyself," or, "All composite forms are without a self." It is the mind of pure compassion and sympathy. The rational basis for human morality is the natural functioning of the mind when freed from self-based aggression and which identifies all forms as its self appearing.

Instead of projecting happiness and meaningfulness onto an external object, the path identifies an entirely different approach—that happiness and freedom arise only in realizing the true structure of the present moment. In that freedom lies the original state of blessedness and peace, or the mind essence. And this realization is what "Zen" points to. Since it is beyond the realm of thinking, it cannot be experienced by a human being. And because it is the true nature of every being, it can be realized by everyone.

27

Falling Out of the Garden of Eden

WAS TOLD A FEW WEEKS AGO that this body, if left untreated, probably has less than a year to live. I asked the doctor, "To die from kidney disease—is it an easy death?" And he said, "Yeah, it's a nice death. You get really tired and foggy and then disappear." That's pretty much how I feel. But then my wife said she would kill me violently if I did that, so it isn't an option. He said that the other options were dialysis and transplant, but to remember that nobody gets out of here alive. A nephrologist teaching the dharma!

If one were to be gifted ten or twenty additional years of life, how could that gift be repaid? What should one do if one were at death's door and then somebody said, "Okay, here is an organ transplant. Ten more years." What do you do with that time? Or to think of it in more general terms, what is it that makes life worth having been lived at any moment? Given the fact that one is alive now, and one is not going to be continuing in life—whether it be a day, or ten years, or fifty years—what is it that makes the appearance on Earth worthwhile?

Of course, for a student of Zen, this is always the question. What meaning does life have, given the impermanence of the stay here? It took the historical Buddha six years of intense practice to uncover the mind essence that underlies the impermanent self. And his insight has inspired spiritual seekers for 2,500 years. He realized that to be alive is to have an unpayable debt. To be alive is to be gifted life; it is not an attainment, it is not something that one achieves. And not only have we been gifted life, but we have been gifted life in a human form. Being gifted life in a human form, we have the gift of a human mind. What makes one worthy of human life is the realization that one does not deserve to exist, and the mind is immersed in gratitude for being alive. And if the mind does not have that in it, then it has not paid back its debt. It cannot appreciate what it is to be here.

The problem that people experience may be called "Falling Out of the Garden of Eden." When you fall out of the Garden of Eden, you fall into the knowledge of good and evil, which is another term for the thinking mind. When the consciousness falls into the thinking mind through the activity of "I am," the thinking activity conceives itself to be an independent self. This is the arrogance of the thinking activity. That is why it loses its contact with the Tree of Life, or the Kingdom of Heaven—because it says, *I am existing of my own power.* "I am" does not like to bow, "I am" likes to prove its worth. "This whole universe exists so that I can satisfy myself"— that is how "I am" looks at the universe. It is all arrogance. One moment of realizing, "I am only here on a visit, and the ability to see, hear, be, has been gifted," and "I" calms down.

When you are sitting zazen, you are allowing the mind to calm down. The body should be relaxed, and the mind eventually comes back home. If you just relax with your mind as it goes through its stuff, if you persevere, if you take on the practice sincerely and apply yourself to detaching from thinking by grounding in breathing awareness, then peace and clarity can be realized. A mind that bows knows that its appearance in this human world is temporary, that aggression is ridiculous, worry is ridiculous, stress is ridiculous, and thinking that your personal life is what this universe is about is ridiculous. When the mind comes home and rests in the light of that which sees it, it realizes that the true being is the awareness.

Can we really appreciate that the sun rises in the morning and makes the Earth warm from 93 million miles away? And that water comes down, and trees grow, and plants grow, and you eat them, and you piss back into the ground, and the piss becomes the tree, and it is all circulating in this one vast universe. This universe has willlessly put together a seed and an egg that grew up into a being that has eyes, ears, nose, and tongue. Out of itself the universe has brought forth this child called you, and this world is your mother. If you are fortunate, you get a notice that your stay here is temporary, and you are humbled. Some people experience that notice as fearful—that is how untrained the mind is. You are gifted life, and the loss of it is fearful? No, that is not the way to be.

28

Waiting for the Prison Bars to Melt

THIS MORNING I WAS THINKING how strange Zen practice is. If you go to church, at least you get a different scripture, a sermon, a choir, and perhaps a piece of cheesecake afterward. If you go to a synagogue, they read a different portion of the Bible each week and give you a chance to pray for your dreams to come true and for your enemies to be vanquished, so it has some benefit to it. In Zen practice, you come and do exactly the same thing every time, and you become, hopefully, pleasantly bored, relaxed, and clear. It's wonderful!

The reason for that is our practice is not about what is going on. The practice is about *how* things are going on. It's not that we are going to learn something new or figure out something profound. As our practice matures and we lose interest in the content of our mind, we become aware of a deeper element in the mind than we are ordinarily aware of. The thinking mind is trying to work out a personal life without including in its calculation the deeper nature of its own existence. In other words, people are living without knowing what the element is within them that is alive, what it is to be aware.

There is rarely a time in life, except during practice, when what one is doing is a pure activity with no self-based purpose to it. Usually, we are doing something for a reason. When we are doing Zen practice, we are not walking in a circle to get somewhere, or to exercise. It is an entirely meaningless activity. But because it is meaningless, when we are walking we have this rare opportunity to realize that we are aware of walking, aware of the body. When we do this, there is more—or perhaps less—than just *I am walking*; there is also *I am aware of walking*. When we are sitting in the zendo, perhaps struggling with the thinking activity, the practice isn't to do something with, or even to calm, the thinking activity—the thinking can be whatever it is. The practice is in creating the opportunity to be sitting here and realize that one is sitting here; to be aware of the awareness that knows that one is sitting and breathing.

For most of us, our lives are founded on the idea that the self resides inside the body. And we think that the self has a name: I am Judy, I am Joseph, I am Sam. Based on this, the thinking mind attempts to work out life. "I live inside this body, and I always like it somewhere other than where I am." We live in a world called "if only" and "sometime."

Then, with great good fortune, we may meet the dharma teaching that says the awareness does not reside inside the body, the awareness beholds the body, and the body does not contain the self. It is extraordinarily difficult to realize something as subtle as that, to see things clearly enough to recognize that when one is walking, the walking is experienced, and that in truth one's whole life is being experienced from a point prior to the physical form and the thinking activity—"prior" in the hierarchy of the present moment. I hope you can catch some flavor of this, that you can realize this principle.

Zen practice is inevitably going to be insulting to the ego. It is not pleasing to the thinking activity, which prefers steak to tofu, which prefers something substantial to dig its teeth into. We have not been informed by our culture, religions, or government that the ego is impermanent. We have been informed by our culture that attainment as an individual is the meaning of life; that idea is an insult to reality. At some point, one becomes aware that life is not happening the way we have been told.

I received an email from a member of the sangha who is practicing at a Zen center in her hometown. They are going to have a ceremony where everybody sews a patched Buddhist robe. In the old days, monks wore garments that were pieced together; some rags were stitched together for one's robe. Looks like it may become a ritual! Nowadays, monks have gorgeous linens and silk brocades with gold rings. She wanted to know if I thought it was a good idea for her to sew a patched Buddhist robe. I said to her, "Your life *is* a patched Buddhist robe, you *are* a garment of consciousness, that is what your life *is*." We are a patched robe—or a child of God, if you prefer—that is how we are existing, and we can never replicate it, we can only realize it. We can't make a picture of it and say, "Now I am a Buddhist."

To be a real student of Zen means the same thing as to be a child of God, and to be a child of God means being humble, being empty. It means, "Whenever I associate with others, may I view myself as the lowest of all. Other people take themselves seriously, I will never get caught in that trap"—this is our vow. And it is so delightful to be free of the pressure of that trap, that we are willing to sit for hours and days, waiting for the prison bars to melt.

So, please understand your practice in this kind of way—its foundation is nonattainment. Know the wisdom that you are a witnessed, an empty-of-self creature—you are witnessed by the light of the awareness that the thinking activity cannot grasp. But when the thinking activity becomes quiet, you know it without knowing it.

29

Stand in the Presence of Ego

MANY PEOPLE HAVE THE IDEA that in meditation they will be doing an activity called "I am meditating." But this is not what happens. Meditation practice is the humbling and quieting of the self. You are put in a situation where the experience of breathing becomes more significant than the experience of thinking. This is the mood in meditation practice. When you take up meditation practice, and you breathe in, you allow the consciousness to meet the breathing instead of meeting only the thinking.

Understand that your existence as an individual is an arc that ends with your disappearance. You are going to go through the experience of no longer existing the way that you think you are currently existing—no matter how many successes you have, no matter how many degrees you have, no matter how many lovers you have, no matter how many lovers you don't have. The noble truth is the impermanence of the stay here, and you come to the meditation hall to practice what it is for the self to disappear. Most religions are not based on examining how it is that we exist. Most religions are based on the existence of something eternal called God who gave a message to humanity. And the message transmitted by the messenger becomes the religion. People feel, "I am participating in something eternal that is outside of me. I am following the commandments of God." These teachings are problematic because they insult the intelligence by insisting that certain things are beyond anyone's capacity to comprehend.

For example, in some religions, there are articles of faith, and you cannot examine these articles with your mind—they must be believed. The existence of God, the existence of a messiah, are said to be beyond mind, so the mind is stuck. You will have to blindly accept that maybe it is true, but you cannot examine whether it is. "Well, just because you can't make sense of it doesn't mean you shouldn't believe in it," and then you get stuck. If you start to question the dogma, there is no answer.

Here, our situation is a little different. Your mind is the only thing you have at your disposal to make sense of your existence, but the mind is being used in a shallow way. People suffer because they are using the mind to invest emotionally in something that is going to disappear—this is the difficulty. The mind is attached, not acknowledging that what it is attached to is a temporary appearance.

What are we doing in Zen practice? We have a teaching we have been given, a guide to help navigate the psychological world. We can see where we are situated in relationship to the thinking activity by taking our eyes off it for a while and putting the inner eye on the breathing activity. It will click at some point; in order to experience the breathing activity there has to be a distance between the breath and the observer. This observing element can be realized only by freeing the self from the thinking activity—that is the whole of the practice. It is not just seeing the breathing, it is also the seeing of the entire body. The activity of the body can be known, the body can be objectified.

Ordinarily, human beings allow the mind to point to the body and say, "I am this," and will not question that deep-seated thought. Usually, it is easier to believe in salvation coming from outside of you when what you are identifying yourself as is bound for dissolution. If you know that is going to happen, your mind invents something that will not be dissolved—but that mind will disappear. Perhaps you cannot grasp that right away, but your way of life should be the humbling of the ego. You should humble and soften the emotional attachment to the things that you are going to lose. When that happens, you will live in a different world from ordinary people, although the structure of your existence is the structure of everyone's existence. The Buddha described the unexamined life as if one were having a party on the third floor of a building that is on fire at its base. This is the human condition: People are trying to fulfill something that cannot be fulfilled. This is the sadness of the human situation. And rather than nobly accepting that truth, people distract themselves.

This universe that we live in has done something inconceivably miraculous. It had created out of itself an incredibly complicated structure—a human being that takes fire, earth, air, and water, and becomes a form that can experience what created it. This is the glory of human existence. You were not created to fulfill yourself as an individual. You were created by the universe producing an organism that could experience what had produced the organism. This world gave rise to you, this world is your source appearing to you, this world is yourself. You may think, "No, I live inside this form." But if you look deeply into this body as it is breathing, walking, thinking, it is just this world becoming this form. This form has the capacity, with its eyes, ears, nose, tongue, and body, to create and experience this universe. No god creates this universe with a will, this universe is created and subsequently experienced by the body and sensory organs.

Maybe you cannot realize that yet, but there is nothing that you have ever seen that has not been formed by your eyes. You are seeing your eyes. Everything that you ever hear is created by your ears—a bird sings out, and you realize, "This is myself; how could it be separate from me? My own ear makes it." This is the great miracle of existence that I hope you come across before your time here is finished. You are going to disappear. Your body has given rise to everything and also performs the function of experiencing it as an object when the personal self objectifies it. "I am existing here together with everything as one body. I am living in overall ultimate oneness." This may be called being born from God.

30

What Is the Address of Love?

SITTING TOGETHER WITH YOU is starting to have an added, touching quality for me. Next Sunday will be the last time I can join you for several weeks or months, depending on how the surgery goes. Fortunately, we are all basically on our own anyway.

One of the problems people have in life is that we have difficulty finding what we are looking for. Everybody wants to find peace; everybody wants to feel loved, or feel love. Everybody wants to feel that their life is meaningful—this is innate. But people don't know what the address is. What is the address of love? What is the address of peace of mind? What is the address of meaning? What is the address, where do you go looking? It's as if someone has a craving for a bagel with cream cheese, and walks into a Thai restaurant and says, "I want a bagel with cream cheese," and the restaurant workers say "Sorry." Then he goes down the block to a Mexican restaurant, "I would like some lox and a bagel." "No, I'm sorry." This is how people are looking.

You could say that the teachings of Zen are the teachings of where the address is. The core is that there is no access to the blessings of life in external objects. These blessings reside within you, they reside within your mind more deeply than the thinking activity. That is the whole of it.

This is the address, and the way to approach it is to free oneself from the thinking activity by cultivating the experience that is without thinking. And that moment is referred to as "the present moment." The experience that is without thinking can be described as breathing in with the full contact of the consciousness with the breathing activity—so complete, so intimate, so pure, that thinking does not break the contact of the consciousness with the body. When you relax, you will find the great affection of the consciousness for its temporary residence.

Today, walking meditation was lovely and slow. What is happening during the meditation is the same idea— you are looking up the address of peace. When you are walking, you are exposing yourself to the full experience of the body walking. You can immerse yourself in it; you are walking, and you feel the body walking, and you are breathing with the full experience of your body while you are walking.

If you relax the body and let go of thinking, there is a deep feeling that permeates your body experience. You will find a smile on your face because it will flow from the consciousness into your being. There is no solution in the thinking activity. I have students and friends who have practiced here for years and are still thinking that the decisions they make are the means for fulfillment. They spend time thinking, "What should I do with this relationship? What should I do with this job offer? What should I do?" Just get it once and for all that the thinking activity cannot bring you fulfillment. Then do what you do.

*

The address for fulfillment and peace and love in the realm of time is this very moment. You cannot find peace by saying, "The future will go this way and that way." If you live your life like that, you will never find it.

What is the meaning of your life? You have to understand the glory of the human body. Seeing into the glory of your existence as this human form is what fulfills you. Being elected president does not fulfill you. Finding your significant other? This thing you call "other" is an impermanent thing, so how can it fulfill you?

The glory of your body is that it has created the universe. The universe that you are experiencing has been interpreted as something existing separate from you. Everything that you experience is actually created by your body—by what it sees, what it hears, what it smells, what it tastes, what it touches, and what it thinks. These are creations of your own body. What you are seeing is your eye. This universe is created by you. And not only is it created by you, but it is also one with you. Every sound is not outside you—it is your body appearing. These things are created by your body and also experienced by your body. It is created as part of yourself and then experienced as being outside yourself. This is the human situation. Can you imagine anything that you can do as an individual that can compare with your fundamental function of having created everything that is? There is nothing comparable. The ego trying to fulfill itself is a mistake.

So, how does a sane person wake up in the morning? By knowing that you are entering a world that is fundamentally one with you. That is how you should live your life. There is nothing outside of you that fulfills you. Have a nice slow walk, and in the walking, be aware of walking. Awaken the wisdom that the world is one with you. Your walking is not being experienced as *I am walking in some alien universe*. You awaken the great wisdom that says, *Your walking and this universe are one event, shined on by the consciousness*. You become a human being through the thought, *I am inside this body*. But now you see that process, you see how God is born into this world. How the consciousness, the source of existence, is born into you. This is something you have to realize on your own; a teacher can only say, "Take a look, this is what you will find." Do not make your life shallow by thinking that fulfillment is outside you—you will never find it. That is the cause of suffering—the idea that fulfillment is external to your being, rather than inherent.

Over these last few weeks my health has been declining. Sometimes, the mind goes to complaining places, or to places of "Gee, are we going to make it through another day?" That is the mind that is going to show up towards the end of your days. You are going to have mental states that have to do with the termination of your being. How will you liberate yourself in the middle of those states? What will be the refuge? If you establish the habit of not rejecting or pursuing mental states, just staying calm in the midst of whatever mental states arise, then you will feel what it is to be kissed by the Buddhadharma, the great wisdom.

How extraordinary, how blessed, how wonderful to have met the teachings that free us from suffering when in difficult places.

31

The Most Precious Thing is You

*T*HIS IS A POIGNANT MOMENT in my life because after today, I won't be able to see many of you for a month or longer.

If you understand life properly, you understand that every day you are a different individual. It is a little hard to understand this because the human mind is not trained or habituated to think that way. That is the reason we study the dharma. The human mind attaches to the body as its identity, as its true, permanent mode of being. And the teaching of our lineage is that this activity of the mind that identifies the body as its nature has a tragic consequence, in that you may never find freedom from fear, can never find true love, and then you die. You can never find the perfection of meaning of your life because you are stuck in a position that is incomplete. It can be said that the dharma teachings are trying to give you an implant, or a transplant, trying to inform your mind that it has been born into this situation, it is not permanently residing here. Interesting, isn't it?

Try to understand, for example, a tree: "Oh tree, what is it like to be born, what is it like to die?" The tree says to you, "I was never born, I have existed forever. I used to be a seed, and this seed was a flow of rain and earth, and it grew into the tree, and the tree made a seed, and this seed grew into a tree, and this tree dissolves into the earth and becomes compost. I am just an activity of the whole universe that flowed through me: the sun, the rain, and the earth. I am a child of the universe." Or ask the flower, "Oh flower, how did you get to be so beautiful?" You'll hear this answer: "I am an activity that is passing along, created by earth, fire, air, and water. I am a child of the whole universe."

The same is true for each one of us. We say, "I am born, I die." But "I" wasn't born. "I" was never born. I didn't appear out of nothingness and then suddenly I existed. No, I just appeared. And this appearing is a temporary activity, and at some point the structure can no longer sustain thinking, which is the birthplace of "I." The kidneys fail, the cancer comes.

Sometimes people commit suicide when they feel that being in this human world is unbearable. The mind has not been trained to be soft, grateful, surrendered, and understanding. The whole universe gave rise to me, my body is created by the whole universe flowing through it. That becomes unbearable to the mind that says, "I am this individual, I am separate from the whole universe." It becomes unbearable, and the mind says, "This body is my self, and this life is horrible, and if I destroy this body I will destroy my suffering." All of these bodies that you see here are going to dissolve. But there is something in us that is different. That is why you should see into this human condition before it can no longer support the life force.

That is why we practice zazen. All we are doing in zazen is facilitating a stillness of the body, allowing the mind to be as it is, and realizing that it is illuminated. There is an illuminating consciousness within us that has, from the beginning to the end, illuminated our being here. And it is never separate from us. We call it our true nature. We call it the truth. Our true nature is born into the human form every day. And because it is born into it, you can know your birthplace, you can know where you were born. "I was born in Cayuga Medical Center." No, Cayuga Medical Center is where I *appeared. I* was born into "I am."

Once you understand the human condition, understanding your birthplace becomes the fulfillment of your appearing in this world. One moment as a human being: "I am hearing the rain." One moment of a Buddha mind: "I am one with the rain—the whole universe one interpenetrating miracle—my true nature illuminates the oneness of existence." I hope that in your life you can have some sense of this. For people to come together in the human world to facilitate the wisdom insight into the divinity of being is a most exquisite thing. Most of the time people come together affirming their individuality, and it is often affirming something that is ultimately not of great benefit.

In the last few weeks my health has been very fragile. And while friends may comfort you, when the mind says, "Uh-oh, this is it," where do you hide? Where do you find the lightness of being in that experience? You will see that you find it in the dharma wisdom. The teachings will come to you at the end of your life when the mind is running, and say, "Just accept the mind as it is. I am illuminating you; I am with you. Just be still."

Unfortunately, you are studying with an old, falling-apart monk. But ultimately the happy teachings are that quieting the mind and being able to contemplate the bodymind as a temporary residence are the most joyous experiences you will ever have. If you are looking for fulfillment in a career or a relationship, you will never find permanent meaning. But just listen to a raindrop and let go of the mental conversation. Can you grasp that when you hear a raindrop, this is the total fulfillment of your existence? What holds you back from that experience? Too busy? This raindrop is one with your body. You are not inside of here, your self is not inside of this body, it is illuminating it. And it is illuminating it in the present moment, not divided into subject and object. The self quiets and the Buddha mind awakens, transcendent.

In two days, I'll be lying on a bed, wheeling into surgery with anesthesia flowing, the mind being anesthetized into nonbeing. When the mind is being anesthetized into nonbeing, what can be said about that? Only silence. Then anesthesia wears off and you come back into human world. "Oh, I am still here." But every day it is the same thing. Every day, the fulfillment of your being is your being.

Why do you hold back your love? Why do you hold back your love for the most precious thing in the entire universe, which is you? Why waste your time trying to find something of worth, when the only thing of worth is your own being? You are never outside the grace of God. The grace of God is the love of the consciousness for itself. But it cannot experience itself the same way an eye cannot see itself. An eye can see everything in the universe but itself, and the consciousness can know everything that appears but itself. God sacrifices its transcendence and is born in this world to find a human being who is willing to sacrifice itself and experience that its true nature is originally the unborn mind. God dies to become a human being; a human being dies to return to God. This is the nature of existence.

Epilogue

All religions are fundamentally deluded. They all worship false gods. All the messiahs, popes, archbishops, deacons, rabbis, ministers, and the rest are also deluded. Any teacher who asserts that one needs an intermediary to approach the transcendent is deluded. Any teaching that one is separate from the divine is deluded.

Any teaching other than "The Kingdom of Heaven is within you" and "All beings are originally the Buddha Mind" (or similar), is inaccurate. No one has ever met God as an object. No one ever received laws from God. The divine is that which illuminates every moment of our existence; hence, as the Psalms say, "Be still and know that I am God."

People whose minds are too clouded to intuit the true nature of mind are subject to being exploited by religions that promise and sell salvation, that promise the forgiveness of their sins for a donation. They are willing to follow unquestioningly customs that are thousands of years old simply because they are thousands of years old. They are willing to believe such illogical things as virgin births, impregnation by the Holy Spirit, that God Herself handed down hundreds of commandments, and that you can be killed or excommunicated for not following these commandments. They need hypocrites who dress in extravagant robes and wave fancy ornaments.

The true human will turn away from all this and submit directly to the calm, shining, inner presence—free of doubt.

About the Author

Yoshin David Radin was born in 1946 to a seventh-generation Lithuanian rabbinical family in New York City. He attended Cornell University, but after traveling around the world, abandoned his plans to become a lawyer and joined a hippie commune instead. He began studying with Zen master Joshu Sasaki Roshi in 1976 and trained with him until Roshi's death in 2014. Radin was ordained by Roshi as a monk in 1982 and an Oshō in 1989, and received the name Yoshin, which means "Light of the Heart-Mind."

Radin founded Ithaca Zen Center in Ithaca, NY, in 1978, and moved the center to the nearby town of Spencer in 1987. Today he gives regular dharma talks there and intermittently at Rinzaiji Zen Center in Los Angeles, his teacher's home temple. Radin's writings, which attempt to express the love between the spiritual seeker of light and the light itself, have been recorded in four collections of songs and spoken-word poems, including *Love Songs of a Zen Monk*. He has also edited two books on Joshu Sasaki Roshi, including *The Great Celebration*, and his work has appeared in *Tricycle* magazine. He lives in Spencer, NY, with his wife Marcia, who is a Zen Buddhist nun.

CPSIA information can be obtained
at www.ICGtesting.com
Printed in the USA
JSHW030351130622
26926JS00002B/4